Sacred Journeys

in a Modern World

Roger Housden

SIMON &
SCHUSTER
EDITIONS

SIMON & SCHUSTER

Rockefeller Center

1230 Avenue of the Americas, New York, New York 10020

Text and photographs copyright © 1998 by Roger Housden

Bibliographic information on the epigraphs throughout the book appears on page 178.
Manufactured in Singapore

1 3 5 7 9 10 8 6 4 2

Library of Congress Cataloging-in-Publication Data
Housden, Roger.
Sacred journeys in a modern world / Roger Housden.
p. cm.
Includes bibliographical references.
1. Pilgrims and pilgrimages. 2. Voyages and travels. 3. Housden,
Roger——Journeys. I. Title.   BL619.P5H68   1998
291.3'5——dc21   97-36455 CIP

ISBN 0-684-83699-8
ISBN 978-1-4516-8368-4

BOOK DESIGN BY DEBORAH KERNER

Acknowledgments

DIANE BERKE, TONY ZITO, AND DAVID AND JOANNE WEINRIB, thank you for all your support in New York, without which that particular journey would never have been so smooth. JAMES PARKS MORTON and everyone I met at Saint John's, your enthusiasm for the project reminded me at difficult times that it was all worthwhile. Thanks to JANE VERNEY for permission to use her photograph of Saint Catherine's in the Sinai after my own had mysteriously disappeared. RANA SINGH opened Benares for me like a book, and PAUL OLIVER, you did the same in the savanna of Tanzania. ORUÇ GENEVÇ, your music sings in me still, and FATIMA, your love and kindness on the road to Konya were an unexpected gift. Thanks to FLORENCE FALK and MICHAEL COLLOLLY for reading and commenting on the text. My appreciation and gratitude to BILL ROSEN, at Simon & Schuster Editions, for helping me to clarify the structure and tone of the book in a way that made it more congruent with what I had to say. I could not wish for a more enthusiastic and supportive editor than JANICE EASTON at Simon & Schuster Editions, or an agent as protective of my interests as JENNIE McDONALD at Curtis Brown. Finally, I owe a lasting gratitude to all the places described in this book. They have shaped me, humbled me, uplifted me, and helped me remember that I am human.

THIS BOOK IS FOR YANN HOUSDEN.

CONTENTS

Sacred Journeys *in a* Modern World

The wise man has no need to journey forth; it is the fool who seeks the pot of gold at the rainbow's end. But the two are always fated to meet and unite. They meet at the heart of the world, which is the beginning and the end of the path.

——HENRY MILLER

The Sacred Journey in a Modern World

*I think everything has a story, and by following our own
individual stories and the stories which face the central
issues of one's life and one's time, if one follows that,
one changes things. The story will do it.*

— LAURENS VAN DER POST

Throughout my adult life, for nearly thirty years, I have regularly dropped my ordinary routine and gone walkabout in remote and untamed regions of the world, or taken myself off along some pilgrimage route that aims at the heart of one of the world's great spiritual traditions. I am not an explorer or an intrepid adventurer; I am not a travel writer looking for subjects; nor can I lay claim to being a "pilgrim" in the traditional sense of the word, since I find it hard to affiliate myself with any one religion. I am an everyday Westerner who carries the gifts and wounds of his time.

I live in a postmodern world marked by uncertainty and unprecedented change. Today the acknowledgment of life as an unfolding and mysterious process is replacing the notion of a rational universe built upon the absolute truths of science. Neither does religion hold a monopoly anymore on what is considered sacred; we are all finding out for ourselves. We are on a journey of discovery, both personally and collectively, for postmodern

1

(quantum) science has given the lie to the myth that we are alone in an alien world; life exists in and through relationship, and we are all in this together.

At the dawn of a new millennium the questions of meaning and identity rub sores into the most well-adapted of individuals, for the once-familiar safety nets of religion, family, and ancestral occupation are no longer there to console us when we fall through our illusions about who we are and where we are going. As the certainties fade, we are becoming a hungry people, and for many, the new apartment with the river view or the BMW just doesn't fill the gap. Yet (as I was amazed to hear Laurens van der Post say recently) even the Bushmen of the Kalahari recognize two hungers: the little hunger for food and the big hunger to join with creation.

So it is an eternal and universal story, then, the one about displacement and the perennial search for home. My personal and instinctive response to this hunger has been to move my body into unfamiliar territory, especially those parts of the world where the primordial wilderness still survives. The wilderness, I have found, stops my mind and returns me to that dimension of being which is also untamed and stripped to essentials. "The empty mirror," the Buddhists call it. The desert reveals the desert in me; the river, the living stream. There are also times, many of them, when I am all too painfully aware of the mediocrity of my own thoughts and the way they have me so easily on a string. I have come to learn that even extraordinary experiences are unnecessary; trials of will or endurance can be just more retaining walls for the ego that likes to star in a movie of its own making.

No, on the best days, just the walking will do, just the river. I may have started out a road junkie, looking for sensations, for adventure. Certainly I did when I was twenty, when I took my first big journey, all the way down Route 66 for a couple of months. Now, though, I don't know. There's nothing wrong with adventure and the wonder of an empty skyline, but I like to imagine I'm there just because that's what I do. I can't help it.

Most of the journeys in this book are through areas of wilderness, but nature is not my only guiding pattern. If you are an educated, traveled, and wondering Westerner, then nature is probably not going to be enough. Our self-consciousness is too refined. Nature has been my bedrock, my ground; out of the empty reaches and lonely tracks, questions have been answered, but they have also spawned still more of their kind. My own sacred journeys have taken me through New York as well as the Sahara, and to Big Sur as well as down the holy Ganges.

I call them sacred whether or not they follow some ancient route or have some holy shrine or city as their destination. What makes a journey sacred today is its ability to stir our own authentic heart. That is the most reliable authority we can have in a world that calls us to assume responsibility for our own life choices. A visit to the place where you met your first love can be a sacred journey, or one to the grave of your mother or father. Wherever its destination, what sets a sacred journey apart from an everyday walk, an adventure, or a tourist trip is the spirit in which it is undertaken. It is sacred if it sensitizes the individual to the deeper realities of his own being and of the world about him——if it brings together the inner and the outer worlds, the physical landscape serving as a mirror for the inner one. I hope this book will help redefine our image of a sacred journey, taking it beyond traditional religious paradigms and setting it in a context that makes it a feasible option for anyone seeking wholeness and meaning in this extraordinary time of the new millennium.

Because it remakes us, a sacred journey is a prayer of the body as well as the mind. Here I tend to follow tradition, where the pilgrim would always travel on foot. Walking engages the body, sets it in rhythm; it offers one's sweat to the lord or goddess of the place; it opens the blood vessels, works the heart, clears the mind, flushes through the flotsam of daydreams. It also has the virtue of taking time, and over time what becomes clear is that the way is the end in itself. "Call off the search!" is the cry of a great nondual master whom I met in Lucknow. "You are the one you are looking for." Yes, but it is only in the walking that we realize there is nowhere to go.

First Journeys

Spiritual homesickness is necessary for us. Sometimes it remains in our hearts most of the time. There are periods one goes through when one is constantly aware of being bereft of something. When this feeling comes we have to watch over our purity and not misuse it. The feeling is itself authentic and is an indication of being near to something. One doesn't really feel deprived until one is close.

— J. G. BENNETT

I was seven when we came to live in Saint Catherine's Valley, that steep cleft in a Cotswold ridge on the edge of Bath, in England. Along the valley lay Saint Catherine's Court with its tiny church. Originally it had been a retreat house for the monks of the abbey in medieval Bath. The old lady who lived there when I was a child used to let me play on the crumbling steps that led to the ancient fishponds made by the monks. The balustrade leant drunkenly inward, grasses and forget-me-nots sprouted round every flaking stone, a fountain trickled in a recess in the garden wall. Beyond the ponds, through an arch cut into the high privet hedge, I had discovered the swimming pool with its changing rooms of privet, one with the name ADAM, the other with EVE carved in formal lettering into its stone step. The pool was always dappled with yellow leaves whenever I saw it. Only once did I brave the risk of the gardener's stick and creep down the stone steps into its chill waters.

A few years later I was out one day walking where I always walked, down across Seven Acres Field toward Bailey's Wood, crossing the stream on the way. Down by the hazelnut trees, bare now in winter, I stopped as I always stopped to gaze at the green band of hills surrounding me like arms and the lone oak tree that used to fill up with sunlight. I looked, and to my surprise and pain, it all seemed suddenly different that day. I could register the beauty, unchanged in centuries, but for the first time I felt an outsider. I was not immersed in it as I usually was. That day, the soft radiance of the Cotswold land seemed unable to penetrate my skin. For the first time, I felt too old for the valley. It was my birthday. I was twelve, and I felt as if I were standing on the edge of two worlds. I turned and went back home, not being able to do what I always did, not quite knowing what to do instead.

In my teens I would spend hours in the chapel of Saint Catherine's, sitting there alone, entombed in cool silence. I would wonder at the monks who had built this stone vault: what they were looking for, why they had forsaken the life of ordinary men to live in this lonely valley. I would wonder at the peace that seemed to descend on me whenever I stayed in that place alone: where it came from, what it was, and why it seemed to leave when I returned to the everyday world beyond the gates. I would gaze in a dream on the little stained-glass window in the tower, the white dove of Saint John descending.

One day I cycled far beyond the valley, some twenty miles to the east, to the stone circle of Avebury. There for the first time I knew beyond doubt that life was not just what everyone seemed to take for granted. Here we were, engrossed in our family and tribal politics, and in the worry over whether we could afford the down payment for a car, and there, right in the middle of our preoccupations, was this staggering testimony to another world, a circle of stones big enough to contain a village, great fingers pointing to the sky for almost five thousand years. Stonehenge was just another twenty miles farther on, but even then tourists crawled all over it from every corner of the earth. Avebury was unknown in the early sixties, and I had the place to myself.

Avebury filled me with awe. It opened a door in my imagination onto a world that stretched back thousands of years. I marveled at the people who had dreamed up this resonator of the spirit, this great circle with a processional walkway some two miles long leading to another sacred hill over the horizon. Who were they? What did they know that we did not? Why had

they gone to such pains to haul these rocks into a configuration so striking that people stood in reverence before them thousands of years later?

The whole area was alive with the presence of a mysterious culture we knew almost nothing about. Long barrows, burial places of ancient chieftains, dotted the hills. Round Iron Age burial mounds, built by the Celts, jutted up from almost every field, topped by a copse of trees. Then there was Silbury Hill, on the edge of Avebury itself, one of the greatest unsolved archaeological mysteries of Europe. Built nearly five thousand years ago, at the same time as the earliest Egyptian pyramids, Silbury is a huge cone of earth that must have taken thousands of men years to erect, and still no one knows for what purpose.

Sitting on the top of Silbury Hill, a crescent moon rising, the chalk land fading into mist along the edge of the horizon, I knew I wasn't alive just to gather the good things of life. No, I was here to ask questions, to decipher the lilt on the wind that I could hear when my ear was turned the right way.

From then on I have always been aware of a wish for something I cannot quite name.

This wish is an inner movement. It has persistently lifted my attention beyond the daily round to face the eternal and impossible questions that are raised by the simple fact of being alive on earth. It has an uncomfortable habit of undermining that part of my mind which seeks to find security and contentment in the things of this world—a relationship, a project, a set of ideas, even a religion. It is an innate intuition, felt in the cells of the body, that we are always on the edge of an awesome fullness of life—quite independent of life's contents—that yet, in our habitual mode of being, somehow evades us.

That which I faintly remember is not of a time past, whether in my own childhood or in the collective myth of the Fall; nor is it somewhere else, in some distant paradise far away from this very material world. I know it to be in the living present, where I too might be and am often not. All our various desires for this and that, all of them stem from this original longing for . . . Plato called it the Good; we could also call it God, or Truth, or Understanding.

We are creatures whose fate it is to have one foot in this world and one in another, here and not here, here and there at one and the same time. I envisage life to be given so that we may stitch the worlds back up without the seam showing. That is what a sacred journey can do. Stitching needs the thread to go in and out, up and down; and since those first journeys, I have followed the thread wherever it has taken me.

Saint Catherine's
in the Sinai

The mountain of Sinai was entirely wrapped in smoke,
because Yahweh had descended on it in the form of
fire.... Louder and louder grew the sound of the
trumpet, Moses spoke, and God answered him with
peals of thunder.

— EXODUS 19 : 18 – 19

I stood in the bus station and stared at the map on the wall. People, mostly men, were sipping tea and gossiping in the morning light. Cairo had been awake for a couple of hours already, but it was early still for me. The map in the Eastern Delta bus station spread from Cairo to Suez and on to the Sinai. A broad road ran from the capital across the Suez Canal and down through the desert to Saint Catherine's—— Saint Catherine's Monastery at the foot of Mount Sinai, bastion of old Byzantium, far-flung jewel of a once-imperial crown, survivor through fifteen centuries of changing fortunes, the coming and going of civilizations, religions, conquerors, and vanquished; and now, as ever, the protector of a bush that once blazed with the glory of the Old Testament God, who delivered his Law there to Moses.

I had always wanted to go there. Byzantium had never been a fossil of the past for me; rather, a mythic land, a Xanadu, a living country of the mind. I saw it as a world on fire with a love of life, a place where value and meaning were neither above nor below but here, in this world, at our fingertips. Ardor, life brimming over, the world of the spirit, present now in the barter and bustle of daily living, in the forces of nature that surround us. I wanted that mirror I imagined Saint Catherine's to be, reflection of Byzantium's fierce and dedicated spirit. I wanted that desert silence. I wanted, too, the truth behind a childhood dream.

The image of the monastery's patron saint had burrowed itself into my imagination decades ago, when my family moved to Saint Catherine's Valley, near Bath. In my teens I would often stroll through the graveyard to the chapel of the old manor house, Saint Catherine's Court, wondering each time at the medieval carving of the saint with her wheel that stood in the porch. I wondered how her fame could have spread even to this hidden valley in the depths of England from somewhere as remote as the shores of Africa, so that even then, seven hundred years later, a boy should grow up in the shadow of her name.

The Court's creaking gate, the overgrown garden have passed into history now. The Court was sold to Jane Seymour, the film star, some years ago; the fishponds are no more, the barns have been turned into houses and sold, a notice tells tourists the visiting hours for the church. Yet the old spell held fast still in the boy who lived in the man, and here I was in the Eastern Delta bus station, faced now with the reality of a broad road that ran through the wasteland of the Sinai straight to the monastery door. A sleek bus with aluminum flashes down the sides and video entertainment already beginning stood right here, on stand number four, ready to whisk me straight to my destination.

Sailing to Byzantium in a video bus. It just didn't fit. No, I had already decided on another way. I did not want to stumble out of a movie at the monastery gates and instantly trade my tourist status for a semblance of hallowed silence. There was another road on the map, a much thinner line that ran from Suez down the middle of the Sinai to Nuweiba, on the Gulf of Aqaba an hour or two south of the Israeli border. There I would find a Bedouin to guide me on the seven-day camel journey through the Sinai to Saint Catherine's.

I wanted to know what it was like to emerge out of the wilderness and see, as thousands had done before me down through the centuries——before roads, buses, maps, and schedules had altered our vision forever——the walls of this legendary place shimmering in the desert haze. To walk through that mythic land was as much a reason for my standing in the Eastern Delta bus station as the monastery itself. I did not seek some impossible journey, a contest with nature's odds stacked against me, the conquering hero striding over the empty plain. I have always preferred strolling to striding, a love affair with the wild more than a struggle. Even so, I was always glad for the purgative effect the desert had on me, the way it drains the psychic as well as the physical excess away. There, returned to proportion, we cast a smaller, truer shadow.

On stand number two there was another, more battered bus that had no driver, no video, no curtains, and no passengers. This was, the man in the ticket booth assured me, the 7 A.M. bus for Nuweiba. Direct. Sure enough, at seven-ten the driver and half a dozen passengers emerged from the tea stalls, and we clattered off into Cairo's morning traffic, past the airport, and out into a sudden and infinite expanse of sand. Not golden, not even yellow, but brown and drab, a forlorn and empty world dotted with concrete bunkers, the occasional car wreck, and billboards exhorting us to drink Pepsi. We did drink Pepsi, at a pull-in just before the tunnel that took us under the Suez Canal to the Sinai Peninsula, on the other side.

To pass the canal was to cross a Rubicon. The same brown plains lay all about us, though without the bunkers and the billboards. Yet everything was different. I could see from my map that we were beginning to cross a large area called the Wilderness of the Wanderings. No mere sand plain, then; no ordinary desert. Immortalized in the Western imagination as the scene of the Exodus, the Sinai was and still is the great crossroads between Asia and Africa, the thoroughfare for conquering hordes, the passage of civilizations. Assyrians, Hittites, Egyptians, Babylonians, Persians, Greeks, Romans, Arabs, Crusaders, and, most recently, the Israelis—all of them have passed back and forth across this bridge of land. None have stayed, except for Isis, who sought here the dismembered body of her brother and love, Osiris—none except a goddess stricken with a lover's grief, slaves, fugitives, and hermits.

The slaves worked the turquoise mines for the ancient Egyptians. The fruits of their labors were the necklaces, pendants, rings, the profusion of blue that adorned Tutankhamen and that glows, to the wonder of millions, in the dark halls of the Cairo Museum of Antiquities. The fugitives, the Israelites, immortalized the Sinai as the land of exile. Apart from the indigenous Bedouin—witness to this incessant coming and going for millennia—

the monks and hermits were the longest-standing residents. No great city has ever left its mark on this wedge of land. It has always been the domain of the monastery and the nomad's tent. It is the empty quarter where God spoke to Moses, where the Ten Commandments were delivered to the Israelites on Mount Sinai—the magnet that has drawn the devout from every country in Europe, the Middle and the Near East, and from beyond the Caucasus to a life of solitude in which they might find their God under the protection of Our Lady of the Desert. For the goddess, in one or another of her many forms, has never forsaken the Sinai. Isis and Hathor in Egypt, Inanna-Ishtar in Mesopotamia, Aphrodite and Artemis in Greece, Cybele in Anatolia and Rome—the Great Mother of all creation was known to the Babylonians as Sin, and from her the desert took its name.

Dreaming, dreaming in the desert land. Big fat wheels, bald tires, driving me down the thin black strip for hours and hours. The sky opens up, mountains fly by, and I roam free through inner/outer space, out of time in this sheet-metal capsule, until all of a sudden we turn a bend and there is the sea, an improbable strip of blue, a shout for life in this land where everything knows to keep silent.

We had clattered into Nuweiba after a mere six hours of driving. The town was a huddle of concrete-ribbon development that stretched round a long arc of beach. The dream stopped here; I was aware now of clammy back of shirt and pants. A mile or so across the gulf, desolate mountains lined the shore of Saudi Arabia. Someone pointed me to a guide in one of the tent cafés that were staked in the sand on the beach. The faint scent of hashish was in the air; a few young Westerners lounged along the bolster cushions; the beach was dreamily quiet—just a couple of fishermen hacking at a squid by the water's edge. The guide was in traditional Bedouin dress, black circlet holding in place a headdress that continued the line of his white flowing robe. He was absorbed in a game of backgammon with a German woman.

When I managed to get his attention, he told me his name was Sliman. As I told him what I wanted to do, his lazy right eye stayed in place while the other one looked me over. Slave of my own prejudice, I immediately felt wary.

"Yes, I will take you to Saint Catherine's," he said, taking a twig and drawing a map in the sand. "I have been everywhere in the Sinai. I was a guide for the Israelis when they were here. First we shall go here, to the Colored Canyon, then to the well of bitter water, then the next day——"

"How long shall we need?"

"Seven days. I shall bring Selman, my cousin, with us. We can leave tomorrow if you wish."

How could I know who this man was or what it would be like to live with him and his cousin for a week? Was a lazy eye to be taken for a cast of character? I didn't know.

"It's agreed, then." The words spilled out of my mouth. "We can leave tomorrow if you can get the provisions by then."

"That is no problem." Sliman's eye was still on the game board. "If you had gone there," he murmured, pointing to one of the woman's counters, "you might have won after all. Yes, we shall go tomorrow. I shall need half of the money now so I can feed my family while we are away."

With that simple exchange the deal was struck. The next morning Sliman drove up to my room in a Toyota truck.

"The camels are at my house," he said, laughing at my surprise. "Come."

We drove over to the Bedouin settlement of Tarabeen, on the outskirts of town. In the yard of Sliman's house three men were squatting round a mean little fire, sipping loudly on tea just poured from a blackened pot. Two camels, lying side by side, turned their heads at our arrival. Another, standing a little to one side, seemed not to notice us. They seemed nonchalant beasts, one of them curling his top lip in a lazy display of yellowing molars.

Around them, bundles and bags and jerry cans——our water supply—— were strewn on the ground. One of the men passed me a glass of tea; the others stirred from their spots in the dust and began arranging the baggage in some semblance of order. It was Selman who offered me the tea, the cousin who was to accompany us. Younger than Sliman, perhaps twenty-five to Sliman's thirty-five, and just as lean, he seemed more inward, his scarf half covering his face, his eyes preoccupied, not seeking outer contact.

In ten minutes, Sliman and I were mounted. Selman took the halter of my camel along with his own and began leading me away from the houses of Tarabeen to the ocher mountains beyond. I was on my way, dipping up and down over a vast expanse of black stones and yellow dust. Selman soon gave me the halter and urged his own camel on from behind, clucking with his tongue. The wind was soft in my face and warm, though it was late November and still early morning.

Then into my thoughts a melody came. Not a memory, but a definite

lilt on the wind. Some sort of Arab pop song. I looked round. We were far already from the last houses of Tarabeen. I peered ahead, turned my right ear to the wind. The sound undoubtedly had its source around Sliman, twenty yards ahead of me. Then I saw it, strapped to the left flank of his camel. A red transistor radio. An Egyptian pop station was throbbing into the desert air. I groaned. Repeating my explanation of the day before, that my journey was a pilgrimage and not a tourist jaunt, I called to Sliman to turn his radio off.

He looked at me in surprise, then switched the music off, turning to yell an explanation to Selman, who spoke no English. We carried on our way without music, but with the growing enthusiasm of the cousins' voices as they debated some topic in Arabic, inscrutable to me. I had misjudged Selman. In the company of his cousin, his interiority disappeared and a voice leapt out of him that approached a scream, punctuated with frequent screeches of laughter. The Bedouin love to chatter, so much so that conversation is the expected payment for any kind of hospitality. It was for conversation, I began to realize, that Sliman had brought his cousin along. Their voices reached the pitch and yell of Cretan widows, and I began to wonder whether the music might not have been better. I hung behind and let the distance swallow their talk.

We were climbing gently between huge rock faces now, along the wadi, an ancient riverbed where here and there bushes grew out of the pebbles in a frenzy of spikes and thorns. A single bird hovered in the canopy of sky. Nothing stirred but us; no sound, when my guides fell silent, but the wind along the canyon. The southern Sinai is a desert not of sand but of bluffs, canyons, and stone plains. My body rolled with the gait of the camel, and I already felt an affection for this ambling mixture of ugliness and grace. There was something strangely endearing about this camel's grunt. A plaintive acceptance of fate. We ambled on for hours, my thoughts returning periodically to our destination. The monastery had always been conceived as a fountain of life in this land of exile and death, and I was on my way to drink there now.

We reached the Colored Canyon sometime early in the afternoon. Selman took the camels round the long way while Sliman led me through a narrow gorge. The relief of shadow, even in a winter sun. The sides of the gorge converged to a pass barely six feet across, perhaps a hundred feet high. The rocks showered light down on us in a hundred shades from purple to pink. Curls of violet, waves of orange, shards of bright red. Fantastical images and shapes. A single eye staring, dark blue. The yellow-and-black fingers, long and gnarled, of some old woman hidden from view. We threaded our way among presences half seen, half felt that loomed from the rainbow nooks and crevices. The fantasies that water had drawn on rock, bright echoes of the time when this canyon ran with a gushing stream. Now all was silent, our feet falling softly over the old riverbed.

We passed through the defile for an hour or more, clambering up rocks where waterfalls once fell, treading on shell fossils, winkles and clams, till the way opened out suddenly before us onto another stone plain. A little way off, Selman was sitting between the camels, who were munching their way through a bushful of thorns. We rode on over the plain till the light slipped away, and Sliman called a halt for the night at the foot of a cliff. The two of them gathered in some brush for a fire. Selman wandered off a few paces to recite his prayers. Sliman confided that he prayed only on Fridays, those Fridays he remembered. I sat for a moment and watched the last light in the west, these two figures in white moving around me, quietly preoccupied with fire, food, and prayer——the rest a vast emptiness descending into night.

Selman rolled a slab of dough into a thick round loaf and laid it in the sand, covered in embers from the fire. We ate the rice and the peas that Sliman had cooked and finished off with a hot hunk of charred bread. I asked Sliman about his family, and he said he had two, having married his second wife a year before.

"It's very good to have two wives, " he assured me. "When you have trouble with one, you go to the other, and so on. They are happy because they each have their own home, and I treat them equally."

My Western sensibilities began to cringe at Sliman's evaluation of a woman's happiness. Yet he did no more than speak the language and perception of his culture. His words were without cynicism or guile, a simple expression of life as it had been lived in this region for centuries. For all the Toyota trucks, the flirting with Western girls on the beach, the tourist dollars, the Bedouin has changed little in the matter of priorities. His culture has always been surrounded by greater powers, and it has always had to adapt to survive. Family customs and loyalty to clan remain, as ever, at the heart of the Bedouin's identity.

Selman reclined by the fire just as he had in the café in Nuweiba, with what I now saw to be a natural grace and ease, not any posture of contemporary coolness. Selman, he told me, was not yet married, which was unusual for a Bedouin in his late twenties. He was reluctant, Sliman said, to find the gift money that Bedouin men normally offer to the bride's father. The cost of marriage was high, and Selman had not yet found the woman who was worth it. The fire faded a few moments after we finished our meal. I took my sleeping bag off into the darkness, leaving the cousins to banter on into the night. Just before falling asleep, I caught the muted strains of Arab pop music.

We moved on early the next morning and arrived at a brackish well by midday. While we were unloading the camels to make lunch, a cool wind suddenly blew in from the east. Clouds gathered, the sun died, rain began to spit in the wind. A few moments more and we were wet through. Gullies appeared all over the plain, the pebbles rustled, Sliman and Selman danced like children. It was raining for the first time in two years. Later, though the clouds remained, the rain died, and we trod on through rust-and-ocher mountains. Occasional thunderclaps, crackles of lightning rippled above.

It was this that I had come for. To breathe this electricity, this iron, into my lungs. The taste of it was on the wind, a sensation on the skin more than dust in the mouth, the raw feel of rock that seemed to color the air a tinge of red. I normally lived in a world of mellow greens and soft mists on the gentle slopes of a hill near Bath, city of warm waters. I needed this rough cut of an unmarked path, the hard edge of a horizon backlit now with jagged lightning. I was glad for this simple act of moving slowly among elements I had all but forgotten in the cocoon of urban Western life.

I wondered occasionally about the thousands of others who had passed through this wilderness before me on their way to Saint Catherine's. The monastery was a stage on what was once known as the Long Pilgrimage. Pilgrims had usually sailed from a port in Italy——Genoa or Venice—in galleys timed to meet the caravans that brought the produce of the East to Alexandria and Jaffa. From Alexandria they would have gone to Cairo, where they would have obtained a right of passage from the sultan. Or they would have gone to Jaffa and Jerusalem, then by mule to Gaza, and on to Saint Catherine's by camel, along the ordinary caravan route.

Everyone in their own style, with their own reasons . . . The first Western pilgrim we know of was one Postumian, whose journey around A.D. 400 was recorded by Sulpicius Severus. Postumian braved all the hazards of travel to seek out one particular hermit on Mount Sinai, a renowned saint

who had not been seen by anyone for five years. He succeeded, though the saint maintained silence in the face of his questioning. In the ninth century two brothers arrived chained together. They had come from France in penance for a murder they had committed, and stayed in Saint Catherine's for three years before returning to Europe, still in chains. In 1336 one Wilhelm de Baldensel rode on horseback from Cairo to the convent in ten days, and in 1860 the comte de Paris went with a caravan of 138 animals and 150 people, to be greeted at the convent by cannon salvos and a procession of singing monks.

By noon on the third day we were lounging among some palms scattered along the wadi. After some more rice and bread, Sliman and I clambered for two hours or more up rock faces while Selman led the camels round the long way. I wished I had gone the long way, unaware that Sliman had not been here for ten years, which he finally admitted to me after we slithered back down two gullies that ended in a sheer drop. We eventually found our way to the rim of a tabletop and started a trek across a broad, flat sand plain, fifteen hundred feet up. It was freezing, a big wind in our faces suddenly, the coarse sand making each step an irritation. As we trod on across this desolate plain the wind bit deeper into my protective layers, pared me down, laid me bare to the lash of the elements.

Was this what I wanted? My feet were sore, my legs were aching, the wind was whipping through me. What price my lust for the wilderness now? This was masochism, pure and simple. Plodding head down through a bare and featureless land for no other reason than for the sake of it. Fear was already at my elbow; it filtered in with the awareness of my limited resources and how easily I could be swept from existence. I imagined Saint Catherine's suddenly, a jewel in the heart of this barren land. I found myself moving toward it now—and me not an orthodox Christian—with the old prayer on my lips, "Lord, have mercy," and meaning it.

We pushed on for hours until we finally reached the far side of the plain and caught sight of Selman crouched by a fire among some rocks below us. He had already made camp and hobbled the camels. We clambered down to join him, my legs barely holding. I threw all the clothes in the bag on my back and lay down by the flames like a child, teeth chattering, vital force gone. Sliman took his only blanket and covered me with it gently.

"Thank you, thank you," I mumbled.

"We are all brothers in the desert," he said without affectation. I felt tears well up as I took in the simple human kinship that survived here still. Ordinary fellowship. No great emotion, the passing of a blanket and a cup of tea. Our shared circumstance not just the desert wind but the common lot of human frailty and kinship, the ceaseless wandering together on the road from birth to death, and maybe beyond.

I awoke in the morning chill and looked about me. Nothing stirred in this wadi surrounded by cliffs the color of mud. I was in the middle of nowhere, my everyday world a distant dream now. I felt restored after a night of deep sleep and no dreams. The world had righted itself again. I lay there, taking the silence in. My friends were moving slowly about their morning chores, bodies hunched against the wind. Selman took his mat out into the sand for his morning devotions. The rituals of fire, food, and prayer, enacted here in the desert just as they had been for centuries.

We struck camp quickly and got on our way, the gait of the camel soon shaking my mood away. We wound our way along crests, looped down through wadis, and spiraled up again. Despite all his protestations and good intentions, it became clear that Sliman and his radio were not to be parted, and we finally came to another arrangement. To their obvious embarrassment, I insisted that I preferred walking to riding. This had a large measure of truth in it, since a few hours on a camel will stiffen anyone's thigh. My principal motive, however, was to be on my own and out of range of the radio. I told them to ride on, that I would follow in their tracks. They shrugged, murmured some words to each other, probably about the peculiarity of foreigners, and made off along the wadi. Eventually, they disappeared round a far bluff. For the first time since we had set out, there was no intermediary between me and the surrounding stillness. As I walked on through the day it entered my pores, settled my mind, and returned me to an instinctual intimacy with the earth beneath my feet, the world of color, light, space, heat, and the wind at my back. Loneliness is an ache in the gut; it cows the human frame, withers our sense of worth. But solitude is food, and I was grateful for it now. Solitude was rejoining me to life, the life in all things, and I ambled on for hours across the sand plains, content to have nothing more to do than place one foot in front of the other.

For two days I followed the cousins' tracks, meeting up with them at noon for an hour or so, and in the evening. They were evidently beginning to appreciate our new arrangement as much as I was, since it allowed them all the radio entertainment they desired. By noon on the fifth day I was following them into Ain Khoudra, an oasis of perhaps a hundred palms.

"How many people live here?" I asked.

"Two women," Sliman replied, meaning two families. Where there was a woman there was a house and family. The men were often away on their camels or selling wares along the coast. A few dozen mud-brick huts stood deserted on the hillside. An older woman and a teenage girl came out of a gate and waved braids and bracelets, the woman keeping a hand free to hold her veil across her face. Two goats raced between us screaming at each other in high-pitched cackles. I thought of the devil, his goat's head. An edge of unease hung over the hundred palms of Ain Khoudra, as if history knew more than my eyes could see. Sliman could tell me nothing, except that the inhabitants had dwindled along with the water, and we moved on, soon to be enveloped again in an expanse of yellow and brown. In the distance a cliff loomed. The cousins were on the summit already, their white robes trailing in the wind against the backdrop of gray.

Ain Khoudra was the only flicker of life that we encountered on our journey. We meandered on through cliffs and canyons that increasingly took on the proportion of mountains. The weather grew cooler by the day. We were firm friends now, and our gatherings round the fire each evening were warm and jovial. They were never happier than when recounting stories, about other strange clients, about their life in Tarabeen, their pride in the Bedouin way of life. For them the Sinai was a world apart, which was occupied, now by the Egyptians, now the Israelis, but which only ever belonged to the Bedouin.

On the seventh day I awoke, propped myself against a rock, and watched the heavy clouds roll by. Sliman was trudging about in a cold wind, collecting firewood. Selman stumbled, half asleep, into his morning ritual. We set off into a strong head wind that blew fiercer and colder by the minute. After a couple of hours, the sun shining wanly, my jacket on, I was frozen to the core. That morning the cousins were riding just a few yards ahead of me. I called out to them to wait and took the blanket covering the saddlebags. After another hour Sliman had to dismount because his camel was shivering and pawing the ground. The animal was so cold it would hardly move. Selman took the halter and tugged the beast into the raging wind, cursing the sky.

On the horizon, the clouds were thicker than ever. No rock or bluff could give any shelter from the head wind. We struggled on for another hour, then huddled between two bushes and made what, I gathered, was the last of the tea. The rice and the flour, they told me sheepishly, had run out the night before. Sliman glanced at me, embarrassed and exasperated. Then he erupted.

"My camel is not happy in this weather," he blurted out. "It is much warmer in Nuweiba than here, and it is still a long way to Saint Catherine's. I must take care of him, he is my living. Also, we have no food. It is much better if we take you to the road. It is only an hour away. You can get a ride to the convent, and we can go back to Nuweiba."

I looked from Sliman to Selman. Both were staring emptily into the sand. I could see it; their minds were set, they would not go on. I was stunned. This land had become my sustainer, taskmaster, inspiration. As cold as I was, I didn't want to be hurtled so soon into the world of the living again. Unaware as I was of the proximity of the road, it had never occurred to me that we had a choice. Yet strangely, I also felt an interest for this unexpected visitation of fate. Suddenly the rest of the day was an unknown. A moment before I thought I was following a plan, and now I seemed to be in the lap of the gods. In the lap of Isis, the Mother of Mothers, Queen of the Desert. From this perspective, I could appreciate the predicament of my companions. It was true, they were wholly unequipped for this kind of weather—light cotton robes and only a blanket to sleep in. They should have known to expect this; they should have known to have brought more food, to have brought at least one knife between them (my Swiss army knife had been on full service). They didn't. I walked over to Sliman and slapped him on the shoulder.

"Come on, then. If we are going to end it, let's get on our way."

They got to their feet, visibly relieved not to have had to face a confrontation. We bent our heads into the wind again. Sure enough, we soon saw a truck edging between the hills. We met the road at the very point where a Bedouin had set up a makeshift café, the only one, they told me, between Nuweiba and Saint Catherine's. It struck me as more than a coincidence, but it didn't matter now. Two Egyptians were sitting by their Toyota truck drinking Fanta. They were delivering Coca-Cola to the village of Saint Catherine's and were happy to take me the sixty-kilometer ride. It would have been a long day had we gone on, and the day after as well. Sliman, I began to think, had underestimated the length of the journey. Perhaps he had suspected as much himself. He turned to me, clasped me in his arms, kissed me on both cheeks.

"Goodbye, my friend."

No other word spoken. An unforgettable warmth between us. I embraced Selman too, rather more formally, and they left immediately. This, then, is what fate had designed for me. I, who had expected to leave all trace of the world behind me at Nuweiba and emerge out of the desert straitened and purified at the monastery gates—I, who had dreamt all this, was to be delivered at the gates of paradise on the back of the mighty Coca-Cola. I clambered among the bottles at the back of the truck and sat back as we clattered down the thin black strip through the stretch of void that moments before had felt like my home.

Saint Catherine's Valley near Bath to Saint Catherine's in the Sinai. One Roger Housden, the latest in an endless procession of pilgrims, adventurers, and inquisitive travelers to stand beneath these fortress walls that guard the head of the valley and the route to the mountains beyond. Long before me, one Lady Etheria, a noblewoman living in Spain around the time of Postumian, had braved all the hazards of travel in her time to come here and visit the site of the Burning Bush, even before the monastery was built. A fragment of her journals was discovered in a library in Arezzo in the 1880s, although the full account of her pilgrimage was in the hands of Peter the Deacon when he compiled his little book *On Holy Places,* in 1157. In her time there was a tower here that served the monks as a place both of refuge and of worship. The tower door was above ground, and the monks would retreat for safety from Bedouin marauders. The tower was still standing when Burckhardt passed this way on his travels in the nineteenth century.

Magister Thetmar, in the thirteenth century, had had to run the gauntlet of the Muslim powers to reach here. Thetmar had arrived before these same walls in the guise of a Georgian monk. On his way, he had passed by Aila Fort on the Red Sea, where captured Franks, English, and Latins (this was the time of the Crusades) were allowed to eke out a living from fishing, a somber warning of the best he could expect if the Muslims saw through his disguise. He was welcomed by the Greek and Syrian monks who were resident at the time.

The same rows of granite blocks that Thetmar must have seen still formed the grim walls, at least forty feet high, that stood before me now. Next to the ancient gate, now sealed, was another, smaller entrance, its iron door closed. I banged on the knocker. I knocked again, more loudly. The blackened door creaked open; a wizened character with straggly white hair peered out. I speak no Greek, no Arabic. I asked in English to see the guestmaster.

"Closed," the apparition rasped. "Tomorrow." The door slammed shut. So much for the time-honored monastic welcome. Tomorrow it was.

I stepped back to stare again at this legendary place whose doorstep I had landed on. Within these walls lay the origins of stories that have shaped the Western imagination for millennia. The bush that once burned with the presence of God grew here still. Mount Sinai, where Moses received the Ten Commandments, stood behind the monastery. The building itself had been here for fourteen hundred years—Mohammed, Arab caliphs, Turkish sultans, Napoleon all placing it under their protection in successive centuries.

Never in its long history had it been pillaged, damaged, or destroyed. Its library of ancient manuscripts, the most precious in the world, survived intact. One of the oldest manuscripts of the Greek Bible in existence, the Codex Sinaiticus, was discovered here. Dating from the fourth century, it was bought by the British Museum in 1933. The monastery's collection of some two thousand icons, many from the early Byzantine period, is priceless. Even now I was standing before a far-flung outpost of Byzantium, for the faith here today is still Greek Orthodoxy.

No one was in sight. Nothing stirred in the fading light but the sound of my own footsteps along the gravelly lane. I walked the mile to the village and withdrew at the sight of the tourist trinket shops to a hotel on the edge of town. A boisterous German group filled the lobby. I made my way to my single room, its one-bar electric heater, and shook the Sinai dust from my shoes.

I sat on the bed, inspected my blisters, then stared all of a sudden into a gaping emptiness. What the hell was I doing here, sitting in this contemporary equivalent of a hermit's cell, the single hotel room, four white walls and tawdry curtains, the banter of a tour group assailing my ears? All this fuss about deserts and monasteries, the living past. Here I was, like everyone else, a tourist in this Arab motel. What was I looking for that couldn't be found in my life in England? That tight little island somewhere off Europe——I too was of that thin-lipped race. I knew like the rest of them what it was like to be one step away from myself, subliminally waiting for a Godot to come and set it all right. There would be no Godot here, either. I sat on the edge of the bed, suddenly on the verge of tears.

I awoke to the sunlight streaming over the walls. I had dreamt of bathing in warm water, a gushing spring. I got up and started out for the monastery. I arrived soon after nine, surprised to see no one else there. The gate was still closed. I knocked on it loudly. It opened a few inches; the same wizened head put its nose round the crack.

"Closed."

"But you said——"

"Closed. Holy day. John Chrysostom."

The door slammed shut. At that moment a group of three people arrived. They knocked on the door, and when the gatekeeper peered round, one of the women spoke to him in Arabic. He closed the door, more softly this time.

"He is going to talk to the guestmaster," the woman told her compan-

ions in French. "Today is the feast of John Chrysostom," she continued, turning to me. "The monastery closes on feast days, but I have connections with the church in Cairo, so we may be let in. I hope so. My friends have come all the way from Belgium to visit Saint Catherine's."

I felt for her friends. A few moments later a portly monk in long black habit emerged, smiling courteously to the Egyptian woman. "How many in your party?" he asked her.

"Three," she said. I glanced at her sideways.

"This gentleman would like to come in too," she added.

The guestmaster ushered me in after the woman's party—in through two more gates, up some stairs, into a room with armchairs and portraits of the Greek royal family round the walls. A young Arab appeared as soon as we had sat down, offered us tea and *loukoumi* (Turkish delight) from a silver platter—the traditional Orthodox welcome to all pilgrims. Outside, the barren Sinai and the world of Islam; inside, a Greek island, tenuous outpost of old Europe, ancient custom surviving intact.

Perhaps there had been some mistake. Perhaps I was in the company of the owner of some stately home fallen upon hard times. Outside, the sun was pushing back the cool shadows. Below us, the church stood in the traditional position, in the center of the monastery, with walkways surrounding it on all sides. We were a level up, on a gallery that continued round half the monastery walls. When Father John offered to show the Belgians round the estate, I slipped off on my own to find the Burning Bush.

It had survived God's electricity well: growing lustily by a wall behind the church, it resembled a healthy, rambling cousin of the blackberry bush, thorny tendrils in profusion. It is the only bush of its kind in the Sinai, and every attempt to transplant it outside the monastery has failed. In the fourth century, some two hundred years before the emperor built the monastery, Etheria, the Spanish noblewoman, remarked in her journal that "it was necessary to go out at the head of the valley, because there were many cells of hermits, and a church, where the bush is. This bush is alive to the present day and sends forth shoots." Etheria's account came halfway between the time of Moses and our own era. Hermits had already lived here for centuries when she arrived. In the Sinai they were free of Roman rule. They dedicated the bush to the Holy Virgin, for in being burned but not consumed it exhibited her immaculate nature. It has been an object of devotion for three thousand years, the manifest symbol of an unearthly event. Whatever the literal truth of its origins, this was a potent bush, even now, and I stood there feeling the weight of the ages.

I wandered on round to the church doors, fashioned by the Crusaders. Here and there an occasional black figure hurried round a corner or disappeared through a door. I walked into a world fragrant with myrrh and frankincense, glowing with the light of candles suspended in bowls from the roof. Solemn faces, dignified figures of saints, gazed at me from the walls, rows of icons, some 150 of them, all of them asking, "Who are you? What do you want in coming here?" I tried to dodge the questions, but they lingered on. Real presences, these figures, summoning the presence in me. I moved slowly, the air thick with more than a millennium of prayers.

Near the iconostasis, the screen that separates the altar from the main body of the church, a monk in swaying robes was pulling the lamps down from the ceiling with a hook, filling them with oil, and sending them back up again. When I asked him where Saint Catherine lay, he pointed me to a golden casket behind the screen.

I stared down at it. This, then, was where she had finally come to rest, the woman whose valley I had grown up in on the edge of Bath. Tradition has it that Dorothea was a fourth-century aristocrat in Alexandria who was converted to Christianity and baptized Aekatherina, the Pure One. During the reign of the Roman emperor Maximinus she is said to have confessed her faith and publicly accused the emperor of worshiping idols. Fifty wise men brought from all over the empire had tried in vain to argue her out of her faith, but she, on the contrary, had converted them, along with members of the emperor's family, to Christianity. She was condemned to death, even so, and spiked wheels were made to torture her. They broke, however, whenever she was brought to them. She was finally beheaded, and after her execution her body vanished. The story goes that angels carried it to a mountain near the present monastery. Three centuries later, some monks of Justinian's monastery found her body, brought it down the mountain, and placed it in a casket in the church. Since her holy relics were brought here, the monastery has always been known as Saint Catherine's.

By the eleventh century, Catherine's story was filtering into Europe. Oil was reputed to ooze from her bones, and she became the madonna of the age when the hermit Simeon took a phial of the oil to the duke of Normandy in Rouen. The oil quickly gained the reputation of a cure for all ills, and Catherine's story swept across Europe in Latin and vernacular prose. Churches and chapels were built and placed under the protection of the saint. In 1148 Queen Matilda of England founded the hospital and church of Saint Catherine near the Tower. The hospice continued until 1825, when it was torn down to make way for Saint Catherine's Docks.

For the next three hundred years after the founding of the hospital and church, money and pilgrims poured into the Sinai from Europe, and Catherine's oil was given to them in phials. The monastery reached the height of its fame in the fourteenth century. Ludolf, a German traveler, in 1341, noted that even the Saracens paid homage to Catherine. In 1390 there were 280 monks, and food was cooked daily in huge cauldrons made in Venice. Largesse was distributed daily to a thousand Bedouin. In 1489 the oil was being collected at the rate of only three drops a week, and that is the last we hear of it. By the turn of that century the flow of oil had ceased, and pilgrims dropped money into the casket in return for a blessing.

Yet what of this perfume that wafted about me now? Not myrrh, not incense at all, but some fragrance of flowers that hovered just in the spot where I stood. I knew the legend, that her remains had always been said to lift a sweet scent in the air. I knew that "the odor of sanctity" had once been ascribed to many saints; that Teresa of Avila was known to have wafted such a sweetness through the room in which she was laid out at death that the windows had had to be kept open. I knew that such stories would only have increased the saint's credibility and the flow of pilgrims to her shrine. Yet I could not deny this sweetness in my lungs, just in this place and no other. I longed to fling open the coffin and ask her straight.

Decorum prevailed. I left the church alone, passing a monk who greeted me briskly with a directness of eye—the first person I felt I had met here, though not a word had been spoken. I had business to attend to, a room to secure. I found the guestmaster back in his office behind a deskful of papers and put my request to him.

"I do not have the authority to let you stay in the monastery," Father John replied. "That is in the hands of Father Pavlos, the acting head of the community. Let us go and find him."

We were barely out of the office door when the monk I had passed on my way from the church came bounding unceremoniously up the steps and along the boardwalk. Father John stopped him, said something in Greek.

"Of course!" Father Pavlos replied in English with a sweep of his arm. "Let him have room number three." Acknowledging me briefly with those steady eyes, he strode on down the gallery.

"Most welcome." Father John smiled a headwaiter smile and led me along the walkway to a blue door. A pastel that would have looked wan in any northern land, here it reflected the clear light of sky, just as it did on a million Mediterranean doors and walls. Father John opened the door and ushered me in. A large brass oil lamp hung from the ceiling, a length of fine old brocade ran over the window. One picture graced the white walls, a print of the famous Christ Pantocrator icon that was in the church. A single bed, a chair, a desk made up the furnishings. I could imagine no better place to be. That alchemical fusion of wildness and domesticity, the mark of the Mediterranean, transposed here to the desert fastness by courtesy of a group of Greek exiles. I turned to Father John.

"Thank you. This is most generous. Tell me, have you been here long?"

"Two years."

"And why Saint Catherine's, of all the Orthodox monasteries you could have chosen?"

"Oh, many things. Though in the end I suppose I was led here. I lived in America for many years, until I took early retirement and decided to give my life to the church. Now, the kitchen is three doors along, lunch is at twelve, and dinner at seven. If you need anything, just let me know."

Father John closed the door and left me with the Pantocrator and the magnificent oil lamp. I sat on the bed, took it all in. I had arrived. Nothing stirred, only the procession of my passing thoughts. Why had Catherine's oil, I wondered, begun to dry up at the very time when a new era was coming upon Europe? At the close of the fifteenth century, the Renaissance was beginning to capture the Western imagination and to place the individual, not king, pope, or even God, at the center of the universe. It was at this time, too, that Columbus swept aside geographical boundaries and in so doing became a symbol for freethinking and individual action. Finally, the Reformation swept across Europe, and Saint Catherine's was forgotten, already a relic of an earlier, more religious age, when faith and thought were shaped by ecclesiastical authority.

Did a flow of oil, or the miraculous in any form, depend for its existence on the willingness of a culture to value it? Does a culture determine reality by its own belief systems? In which case, allow for miracles to happen, and they do; preclude the possibility, and they don't. Certainly, for the last hundred years or so, the magic and wonder of the technological age has eclipsed all earlier enchantments. Now, though, books on angels top the best-seller lists, oracle systems from all over the world are sold along Main Street, and people are beginning to walk the old pilgrim routes once more. Perhaps miracles are possible again. This time, they are confirmed not by the seal of ecclesiastical authority but with the conviction of individual experience. And though the extraordinary can happen again now, primacy is given as much to the miracle of the ordinary, the sudden revelation of beauty and wonder in the entirely familiar. Free of the constraints of traditional authority, the religious impulse, innate to humanity, survives and thrives now in finding individual expression.

Outside, someone was hitting the hard earth with a pick. An electricity generator was throbbing. I had been vaguely aware of it since entering my room. Now, it suddenly stopped. Four white walls, just like the hotel room I had left earlier that morning. Yet I was at home in this one. It was all in the eyes of Christ Pantocrator, Ruler of the World; they seemed to suggest that a tender pain accompanied wisdom—full of feeling, and at the same time, beyond it. I felt the pathos of my own predicament there: a Western individual with a religious impulse, yet without a religion, drawn back to the very roots of the Christian tradition—Saint Catherine's in the Sinai—drinking in its austere beauty, its potent air, the old Europe and the old religion that was still in my blood, all the while knowing I did not belong. For all the difference in the worlds we inhabited, I felt a certain kinship in that moment for the displaced of the developing world, those in Asia and Africa who had grown up in traditional cultures and who were having to adapt in a hurry to the incursion of the global economy.

That night, around two-thirty in the morning, I was woken by the scuffing of stones and the banter of French voices calling to one another in the dark outside the monastery, beyond my window. Lying there in my irritation, I remembered what the German party in the hotel the night before had been talking about. They had been discussing their experience of walking up Mount Sinai in time to watch the sunrise. Some of them had been surprised—disconcerted, even—to find a refreshment booth at the top of the holy mountain selling Coca-Cola at extortionate prices. Since it was a steep climb of three hours up the mountain, the vendor never lacked for customers. All the organized tours had the dawn trip up the mountain on their schedule, and sure enough, soon after the French I heard American voices, before resorting to earplugs.

I decided then and there not to follow them. Sharing a mountaintop with a hundred others, their guides and fifty flash cameras, was not my idea of a dawn vigil, even if it were true that Moses had been there before me.

I awoke the next morning and emerged onto the balcony to find the ground level and church already teeming with tourists. Video cameras whirred, shutters clicked, syllables from a dozen languages clashed and vied for airspace. Japanese, German, French faces looked up at me and wondered how I had got here, on the balcony closed to visitors. The fifteen or so monks were all on duty—crowd control at the church door, guarding the icons, showing groups the Burning Bush, selling postcards from a crowded booth.

"We need these people," Father John told me when I asked him how he felt about this daily invasion. "Apart from a small UNESCO grant we have no income other than our tourist trade. Tourism is also a way to be of service to the world at large. Saint Catherine's is not ours. It is not just a monastery, but one of the great cultural and historical centers of the world. Our duty is to preserve it for the benefit of all, and at the same time to find the right balance. The Egyptian government sees us as a source of foreign revenue, and are pressing us to stay open more hours, but that would endanger the tradition of monastic life. Saint Catherine's has always had a delicate relationship with the Muslim rulers of the land. This is why we have a mosque within the monastery walls, a token of goodwill towards those who are stronger than us."

The transformation that happened on the stroke of twelve was extraordinary. Everyone vanished, back to the sleek silver buses at the end of the drive. In five minutes, Saint Catherine's had returned from a tourist mecca to a contemplative community. The shop shut; a monk struck the *semandron,* the summons to prayer; lean black figures shuffled through the church door; silence fell.

Toward the end of the afternoon siesta a young monk of ample frame introduced himself to me as Nicolai, from London. On completing a psychology degree, he told me, he had no ambition to make anything of himself in the world, and busied himself with odd jobs for a couple of years. He had always been attracted to Orthodoxy, and decided to go on a journey to Jerusalem with a friend. From there he came on to the Sinai and Saint Catherine's, was baptized, and had been here for eight months.

"I have finally come home." He beamed. He went on to describe the world's monasteries as arks of refuge in the midst of the world's greed and egoism, of the sin that was ingrained in our bodies and minds, of the force of evil that stalked the land. I listened, hearing echoes of the Middle Ages. Already, this young man spoke with an intensity that allowed for no alternatives. Perhaps I, on the other hand, suffered from too many.

Nicolai led me to the room where I had first had tea with the Belgians. Another young monk, in his early thirties, was sitting with a frail old brother with a long white beard.

"Father Angelou is the oldest member of our community," Nicolai said, introducing me. "And this is Father Justinian, from France."

Father Angelou rose uncertainly to his feet and flashed a wild, childlike smile. "You are from England," he exclaimed. "And what do you think of Oscar Wilde?"

I didn't know what I thought of Oscar Wilde. No one could have been further from my thoughts. Angelou was laughing, and I laughed with him. Unconcerned that I had no ready answer, he almost collapsed back into his chair, content with having asked the question.

I asked Justinian where he was from. He had come from Royan, where he had been living in the Orthodox monastery for some years before deciding his calling would be better served if he left his native country.

"Exile is an important theme in the Bible," he explained, "and usually in relation to the desert. The desert is a place of purification. It is also where you are likely to be beset by devils. It represents for us both the land of truth and the place of deception and danger. It has always been accepted in the monastic fraternity that some members will succumb to the dangers here, and even go mad. In the early period of the Desert Fathers, there were whole monasteries and churches set apart for monks who went off the rails."

Justinian was alive with his theme; an intelligent passion edged his words. He had been in the Sinai for two years, and we talked animatedly about the desert and its deceptions until the thwack of the *semandron* announced the afternoon service.

This was the short version of worship, some forty-five minutes. The main service had started at 4 A.M. and continued to 7. I followed the monks into the church and stood at the back while the community raised its somewhat tuneless voice in liturgical chant. A monk floated about lighting more candles; another swayed a censer of frankincense; Father John read from a huge Bible that stood on a lectern. An informality—whisperings, nudgings, the occasional smile—mixed strangely well with the surrounding weight of history. I was glad for their ease and spontaneous Greek style, glad, even, for their mumbled, discordant singing. These monks wore their human frailty, their humor, for all to see and share in. I felt glad to be among them, warmed in the company of brothers, men of passion and simplicity, for all their fears of temptation and women.

In the days that followed, I was content to sit for hours on my bed, letting the stored silence of old walls seep into my mind. I watched the tourists in the morning, went to the library with Father John in the afternoon to pore over the rows of ancient manuscripts, shelves of books on medicine, mathematics, astronomy, philosophy in Greek, Aramaic, Hebrew, Arabic——the entire body of knowledge of the ancient world stood here gathering dust. I came to enjoy the company of Father John, his brevity of sentence, his quarter smiles. I learned that he had been married twice, that he had worked many years for the Onassis shipping line, that he had installed a fax as well as a phone in the monastery office. He told me that in his opinion the community had a great blessing in Father Pavlos as their head.

"He is the highest person in rank here below the archbishop, but he insists on having the poorest room. He is always giving food away to the Bedouin, and the local children always know where to go if they want a piece of chocolate. He serves the monastery with his every breath."

Even as I felt my increasing love of the rhythm around me, the sense of people having given over their lives entirely to a spiritual ideal, the long spans of silence, I knew that the old way, the mystery enacted daily behind those great doors of cedar, would forever evade my more contemporary cast of mind. On my last day, Father John escorted me to the door. Shaking my hand, he gave me Saint Catherine's calling card, and said, "You can fax me if ever you want to come again. You will always be welcome."

I thanked him, he gave me his quarter smile, and we turned to our respective worlds.

I passed through the outer wall and came face-to-face with Father Pavlos.

"What kind of world are you returning to?" he asked.

"One in which I am not always sure of my place."

He smiled. "I do not know the value of my life, to myself or to anyone else. I know that I have no choice, though, except to follow my calling, for better or for worse. And my calling has brought me here. Whether it is for any greater good, only God will know. All I know is that I am in the right place. I wish the same for you."

"Thank you, " I replied. "Thank you."

This man before me now, a clutch of spring onions in his left hand——he was there, on his own firm ground. My calling, I felt in that moment, was to stand on that ground wherever I went. We shook hands, stood for a few seconds with each other in silence, and parted——he to his monastery, I to face the taxi drivers at the end of the road and some stiff bargaining.

Divine
New York

O n the runway at JFK, a large red butterfly——a majestic, I think——fluttered up and down against my window, my first sight of New York on landing from London. I simply tell what I saw there on the Kennedy runway. Minutes later I was on the blue line to the immigration desk.

"Your date of birth goes in the line below, not that one. Let me tell you what it's like for the checkers." The large woman in navy with dreads leaned back in her chair. "None of them are under seventy-five. They sit in a room with no air, no ventilation, and a lot of smoke. They don't like to look twice at the same line. So you put your date of birth there."

So I do, both of us smiling. An hour later I am sitting in a gridlock that seems to be set for eternity. Across the highway in Queens a row of stores proclaims the New York diversity:

WEST INDIAN AND AMERICAN GROCERY

THE I AM SANCTUARY: THE SOCIETY OF ST. GERMAIN

NATIONWIDE MATTRESS STOREHOUSE

AL KHOEI BENEVOLENT FUND

What interest could he ever arouse there? I thought; Saint Germain, that most mystical of mystics, sandwiched between mattresses and sweet potatoes. But why not? Isn't that the whole point? Isn't that why I am here, on a pilgrimage through New York to the Cathedral of Saint John the Divine, because this city, of all cities, challenges the gulf between sacred and secular and celebrates the spirit right in the heart of the marketplace? You get what you look for. I know New York is a tough place; I know people are murdered and abused here every day; I know it is a world of concrete canyons, towering monuments erected in honor of greed and power; I know about the holes in the street, the piled-up garbage, the noise, the intensity that has you wired all hours of the day. I know all that; I do not deny it. I have been here before. And I know New York is something else besides.

The point is, the human spirit sings out even more loudly in the face of impossible odds. I know of nowhere else in the world where so many different cultures, races, and interests have been thrown together on one tiny plot of land and not only managed to avoid killing one another off but actually succeeded here and there in transcending religious differences and reaching for a language of the spirit beyond the limitations of race and culture. I know of nowhere else in the world so thoroughly secular and market-led, and yet where so many individuals are genuinely seeking to give the human spirit new forms of expression within the context of a busy everyday life. New York has always been the ultimate testing ground not just for new products but for new visions. It may sound good on the West Coast, but will it stick here? If it's too soft, it just won't take the heat, and let's face it, the hard school of the real world is the litmus test all over the globe now. If a sense of the sacred is going to survive, it will have to make it in New York. Saint Germain seems confident enough about his chances.

Naturally the next morning I am on the Staten Island Ferry to get a view of the skyline and the Statue of Liberty. I don't care how many plastic replicas of it are on mantelpieces all over the world. However much her name has been slurred by the iniquities of market forces, brutal repressions, greed, hatred, and envy, that Lady who greeted all those people off the boat on Ellis Island and who endures now hordes of tourists swarming over her feet and her light still has something to say. In fact what she says is even more poignant for all the mud in her eye. She holds even now a mirror to each person's vision of the possible, their image of what they and America may become.

Freedom in America tends to mean freedom of the individual to create a life and live it as they see fit. Our understanding of that freedom is evolving along with the experiment that America is herself. Not so long ago that skyline was still the land of the latter-day rustler, the corporate raider of individualism run riot. More recently a major offshoot of individualism has been a search for identity not only in outer success but in self-understanding and self-management. Even the businesses that inhabit those columns are paying out millions of dollars to have their managers become more able to access their inner resources. More recently still, there is a burgeoning wave of interest in congruent living, where outer actions are a reflection of deeply held values. "Values" is a hot buzzword among business consultants right now.

On that ferry to Staten Island I look back at the skyline and see a country where more individuals than anywhere else on earth are committed to freeing themselves of hand-me-down thinking and outworn beliefs, to empowering their lives with consciously chosen values that enhance not only their own lives but the lives of others as well. The freedom of the human spirit is what our Lady stands for, the impossible yet necessary dream of building heaven on earth. Not with the help of Congress, though. These are individual dreams, community dreams, grassroots dreams. A lot of Americans are having them.

The shoe-shine boy on the ferry is white, in his sixties, and wearing a cap with LETHAL written on the front. There is a smile in his eye all the while he cleans my shoes. Off the boat and back in Manhattan, I run into a bull with definite attitude, a bronze bull pawing the ground at the start of Broadway like he's ready to take the whole city by storm. Perhaps he lives out what all the suits in the financial district feel inside. On the corner of Broadway and Wall Street a mobile Hare Krishna lunch stall is doing brisk business

with falafel and vegetarian kebab to go. Over the road in Trinity Church a lunchtime meditation is under way. I peek in and see that it's packed, everyone in gray and pinstripe.

A few blocks away, by the World Financial Center, I find my own place to sit, a pink granite bench facing the Hudson and the Quotation Fence, an iron grille along the waterfront with lines of poetry etched into it with gold leaf lettering. *Passionate city, mettlesome, mad, extravagant city . . . ,* wrote Walt Whitman, who loved to walk through New York more than down any country lane. Behind me Roy Lichtenstein's great splash of Byzantine blue lights up the Financial Center's doorway. It's quiet here, in the center of the hub, and I gaze over Whitman's words through the yacht masts to the water beyond and a low rippling with a wind rising softly. Over the way, people are eating their lunch in the maze garden on a circle of wooden benches.

I have an appointment on the granite bench with Jack Goldstein, formerly president, for ten years, of the OMI Corporation, the second-largest bulk shipping company in the United States. "You have to meet him," a mutual friend had urged. "He'll blow any preconceptions you may have about top executives." Jack, now chairman of the board, strolls up exactly on time and joins me overlooking Walt Whitman's words.

Some years back, Jack tells me, when he was vice president of another shipping company, he knew that he wasn't happy but didn't exactly know why. His dissatisfaction grew into depression and he went into therapy. In 1985 he went to a workshop led by the healer Bernie Siegel. Siegel had everyone go into relaxation and draw a picture while listening to the Pachelbel Canon. Jack was surprised at his own drawing: he had drawn himself in the air with his arms open and seven stripes on his chest, floating above a budding flower on the earth that had seven leaves.

Soon afterward he took up yoga for his health, and during one session the teacher did a relaxation exercise. Jack imagined himself floating up to the ceiling, holding his sister's hand, and inexplicably began crying. The next night he had a call to say his sister had died. Rabbi Gelberman, who had married Jack and his wife twenty-one years before, officiated at the funeral. After discussions with the family, he noted that Jack's sister was fifty-two years old and had been married thirty-four years. Each pair of numbers added up to seven, and for him that meant it was her seventh day, and time for her to rest.

Soon after the sevens entered Jack's life, he became president of OMI. From then on the number seven started appearing everywhere, leading him to make intuitive business decisions that, as a trained economist, he had no logic for, except that whenever there were options and he took the one with a number seven in, it worked. Then he moved his office and his new telephone number was full of sevens; he moved his home to an address with the number seven. Jack, by his own admission, was a hard nut to crack. He had never imagined that the world worked in any other way than along rational lines. This number seven business had him spooked for a while, till he finally decided that numbers must be the only way for him, an economist, to be shown that there are other forces at work than the linear and visible.

"I gradually began to live life with a trust I had never known before," he went on. "It's as if things are looked after from another level. When I joined OMI, in 1986, the firm was in a bad way, on the edge of bankruptcy. Then we received a call from a broker's in Europe saying they had a ship for sale. It's name was *Settebello,* 'beautiful seven.' We bought it immediately and it turned the business around."

Jack Goldstein was honored recently by the unions as the industry's most compassionate employer. His position obliged him to make tough decisions, and he did what he had to do for the good of the company. At the same time he tried to ensure that people were looked after. "Arjuna, the hero of the Bhagavadgita, is a good role model for me," he says. "You know, he has to do his duty and go to war, but he doesn't bear his enemies malice. He knows that Krishna is planning the whole show. Now, I'm not a Hindu, I'm a Jew, and not a very observant one, but I know beyond any doubt that my life is guided. It may sound strange, but I tell you, I just know that I don't have to think up what to do. I follow what's in front of me, follow the signs."

I looked at him, a gray-haired chief executive in somber gray suit, and remembered not to be fooled from now on, the human spirit having all kinds of guises. Jack's story gave me pause, and I wandered up Broadway immersed in my own thoughts, brought out of myself only by the sight of four cast-iron totemic shafts, maybe thirty feet tall, rusting, soaring up from a lawn among trees and benches on the edge of Federal Plaza. *Manhattan Sentinels,* Beverly Pepper called her work, and a plaque tells how, in the past, forms like this served as monuments to spiritual devotions. Today, says Pepper, she sees them as a celebration of human aspirations and continuity. The building behind Pepper's work houses the U.S. Immigration and Naturalization Service, and a global crowd throngs outside in hope of living those aspirations. A tramp walks by with a metal detector scanning all the subway grilles for the dropped quarter or dime. I remember not to be fooled by the disguise.

Off West Broadway a few blocks north, a man-sized cardboard carrot with a big smile stands on the sidewalk holding a board scrawled with the message GOD IS LOVE. Next to it is an open doorway with the sign LUCKY'S JUICE BAR. The counter is stacked with vegetables and alfalfa sprouts in seed trays. All the customers are laughing and joking with the three assistants, all young and hip. A large banner with a picture of Bob Marley on it flutters over the proceedings. Photos of saints are pinned on the wall by the door, along with press cuttings extolling the virtues of Lucky's juice. I sit on a bar stool and talk to Lucky over a carrot-and-beet. Lucky is middle-aged cool. There's no rush in his bar; this could be Marin County, except it's West Broadway and Lucky's from Brooklyn. "I couldn't get a job," he tells me. "Too old, I guess, so I went into business. I've always loved juice, and it's a good area, the best, a lot of pretty girls; but it's a kid's thing, really. I'm doing it for my son. He runs it mostly. I leave every winter for Mexico."

I remembered suddenly how James Parks Morton, the dean of Saint John's, had responded when I had asked him on the phone which places in New York were sacred for him, apart from churches. His first answer was the pizza place across the street from the cathedral. "It's just the atmosphere," he had said. "It's been in the same family for decades. They really care about what they do and how they do it. I have felt cared for there as much as I have anywhere."

It was nothing Lucky said, nothing particular about the decor, but I have returned often to his juice bar since then. The place has got soul; you step through that doorway and you slow down and remember you are a human being.

The next morning I had an appointment with the dean in his office at Cathedral House, up on Amsterdam Avenue. I'm in New York this time to take part in the Festival of Saint Francis at Saint John the Divine, the celebration in which animals of every imaginable kind are brought into the church, along with five thousand people, the Paul Winter Consort, dancers, light shows, and representatives of all faiths. The festival was a few days away still, and I wanted to meet the man who, as dean for twenty five years, had made the cathedral what it is.

Walking into his office was like stepping into the rooms of an Oxford don. The windows were neo-Gothic. His desk was littered with papers, a few books, a head of the Buddha, wooden articulated snakes and lizards. Another table was stacked high with piles of books and magazines. A worn leather armchair faced the desk. James Parks Morton is a large man in every respect, a Renaissance revival, passionate about everything, bursting with ideas, always pressing for the larger picture. His vision of a modern cathedral draws on the early medieval model, when the church was at the heart not just of religious life but of social, cultural, artistic, and philosophical activity as well. It is largely due to his efforts that Saint John's is a living example of that holistic model.

"You know," he began, heaving himself into the chair behind his desk, "in doing what I've done here I've really been expanding a tradition that was always a part of the history of Saint John's. The prophetic tradition, that is, action in the world. Look at what Bishop Manning did here in the nineteen-twenties. He had a whole slum dismantled and reerected in the nave so that everyone going up to the altar for Communion had to pass through it. The interfaith dimension was here too, if only symbolically. The plans for this cathedral began in the eighteen-eighties, when immigration into New York was at its height. The diocesan leaders envisioned their cathedral as 'a house of prayer for all nations,' and the seven Chapels of Tongues which finally curved round the eastern end were dedicated to the major groups of European immigrants at that time. Did you see the imperial Shinto vases? They were given by the Emperor Hirohito in the thirties. And the menorahs on either side of the altar—they were a gift from the founder of the *New York Times* in 1925. What I have tried to do is build on these symbolic gestures with practical action, though it hasn't always been easy. I was almost crucified when I first had a Shinto ceremony in the cathedral. There were people claiming that the altar had to be reconsecrated, that we had committed heresy.

"That, you know, is what I really care about—that we have established a pattern for what a cathedral is about in this era. At the beginning people thought the kinds of things we did here were nuts. Now they are being done all over. The Festival of Saint Francis is celebrated in a similar way to us now in dozens of cathedrals in America and elsewhere. The arts, the environment are not just seen anymore as sexy programs to pull in the young; they really are the only way you can worship now. They are natural as breathing. I don't see how you can have a cathedral today without artists in residence. It isn't a nice idea, it's fundamental. I tell you, one of these days we shall have drums recognized as crucial to the liturgy. Indigenous peoples are our teachers now. Many Anglicans are recognizing all this, though some, like the present archbishop of Canterbury, are running a little scared."

I tried to imagine the dean at Lambeth Palace in private audience with the archbishop. I couldn't picture it. Of course, Saint John the Divine has all the traditional statuary, iconography, and liturgy of the Presbyterian/Anglican Church. But what, I wondered, would the denizens of Lambeth make of the huge quartz crystal in the aisle, the giant ostrich egg, the 100-million-year-old fossil, all celebrations of God's creation? Or the stained glass windows portraying Hippocrates, Immanuel Kant, and the Ottoman jurist Abu Hanifah? What other pulpit has been occupied by the Dalai Lama, the mayor of Jerusalem, the governor of New York, the president of the Czech Republic, celebrated environmentalists, writers, artists, and politicians? Which other cathedral gives studio space to writers and artists—including a high-wire artist? Or has a resident dance company, a photography wall, and galleries featuring exhibits by young artists? Then there is the Gaia Institute and the Lindisfarne Association, bringing together poets, scientists, and religious leaders to discuss broad issues not dealt with in single disciplines; there is the Temple of Understanding, founded by Pope John XXIII, the Dalai Lama, Jawaharlal Nehru, Anwar Sadat, and Albert Schweitzer to explore the common ground between the major faiths; the homeless project; the recycling project; the environmental work; the . . . It goes on, and the mind boggles.

I wanted to know which influences had led Morton to such an all-inclusive vision.

"Alexander Schmemann was an important mentor for me. He was dean of Saint Vladimir's, came out of Saint Sergius in Paris. I met him in fifty-eight, and in nineteen sixty he invited my wife and me to his summer hideaway in Canada. We have been every year since, so I have been soaked in the Orthodox view of the Eucharist. Then I got very interested in Hasidic Judaism in Chicago in the sixties, and Pir Vilayat Khan introduced me to Sufism, which blew me away. See, it's the mystical stream which informs all these traditions. It's a perennial, universal thing."

"Do you find it in the Anglican Church as well?"

"Of course, and I'm happy where I am. I don't need to become Orthodox or Jewish because I value their traditions. The advantage of Anglicanism is that it's a kind of Quakerism with nets. You know, T. S. Eliot said that Quakerism was like tennis without nets. Well, Anglicans have that gamy, sporty element that you won't find in Roman or Orthodox churches; they're far too serious. I like the membrane metaphor, something that keeps the form together but you can go in and out. That's Anglicanism for me, so Sufism and the like seep through my membrane.

"Another big influence was Geoffrey Beaumont. He was chaplain at Trinity College, Cambridge, where I went after Harvard. Marvelous man, always in the West End nightclubs with a fag hanging out of his mouth. He had been a naval chaplain before, and his rooms at Trinity would always have odd characters from those earlier days sleeping on his floor. One night we were drinking gin in his rooms when he turned to me suddenly and asked, 'James, how much do you think about lizards?'

"'What?'

"'Lizards. How much do you think about them?'

"'Well, can't say I do, much.'

"'They matter. They matter to God. You'd better think on them.'"

My eyes fell on the lizard on his desk.

His secretary announced, "There's a call on line one, it's James Adams." The dean motioned me to shut off the tape and picked up the phone.

"A window to commemorate the victims of TWA 800? That's a great idea, James. You mean under the jurisdiction of the U.N.? That would be the only way for it to happen. Jerusalem a world city of faiths under the jurisdiction of the U.N. That is a wild and brilliant idea. I'll phone Boutros right away. They're meeting tomorrow in Washington, aren't they? It will save Boutros' ass if he can pull off something like that. Okay, James, I'll talk to you tomorrow."

He turned to look at me. "Would you believe it? That guy is eighty-eight years old. He is our biggest sponsor. There's enough life in him for ten people."

"There's enough life in you for a dozen." I laughed. "What are you going to do when you leave here in December?"

"We're going to start the Interfaith Center of New York," he answered. "We just need a few more serious backers. Among other things it will have an international exchange program so priests and monks of different faiths can experience the value of other traditions. Then we will have a training program in conflict resolution, linked with a university here, so that clerics can help in areas of religious strife. It will be a sort of living museum of world faiths. The whole idea is to challenge the heresy that any one way is the only right way."

"Is there anything else you would have liked to achieve here at the cathedral?"

"Well, I would have liked to be God . . . No, I'm happy with what we have done here, though I am passionate about seeing the cathedral completed. As you know, the construction has been an ongoing process for the last hundred years, stopping and starting depending on funds. We have the designs; Santiago de Calatrava won a competition we held a few years ago; all we need now is a hundred million dollars."

Another call on the line, and time to go. I shook his big hand, which was curiously soft. "See you on Francis Day." He beamed; then he was absorbed in some conversation about television rights for the filming of the Saint Francis celebrations. Outside, a sculptor was working on the statues in the great west doorway. When I called up to him he replied in a voice more English than my own, inviting me to join him up on the scaffolding. There among the pigeons and their droppings, Simon Verity explained how in 1988 he won a competition for sculpting the figures of the cathedral's western facade, the main entrance, on Amsterdam Avenue. America has no tradition of stonecutting, so the competition was held in France and England. Simon, who repaired the thirteenth-century statues at Wells Cathedral in England, was chosen along with Jean-Claude Marchionni, a stonecutter from France.

"This job has been a true rite of passage for me," he said, chipping away at a square block with pencil marks on it as we talked. "I have had some difficult years since I have been here, and that is reflected in the figures I sculpted during that time. You see the deep shadows they cast, the sense of crisis in their faces. Things are better now, and the figures I am working on at present are lighter, freer. If you look at the sculpture of any great cathedral you will see differences that are clues to the mind of the sculptor. The dean has given me complete freedom to interpret the figures as I feel moved to do, and that is a real blessing."

I wondered how he could stay up there all day long under a cloudless November sky with the temperature around zero. "It just comes with the job," he told me, "like the pigeon shit. You get to like pigeons eventually." He laughed. "I guess the real reason is that for me my work is my altar. I'm not religious in the conventional sense, even though I spend all my time with biblical figures. But the work, there's something primal, sacred about the activity of shaping stone. I've always thought that sculpture was close to plowing. Like a farmer, you separate the stone from the earth."

Verity completed his work in 1997, though the work of finishing the cathedral continues. There is something profoundly dynamic about the idea of a cathedral in process, especially in New York, a city founded on the idea of the new, its very patterning urging it to invent history as it goes along. Then it struck me how apt it all was, how this was it, the New Jerusalem in the making, the impossible dream imagined by Saint John "the Divine"——"the Theologian"——in whose name all this labor was being undertaken. "Impossible, but do it anyway": I can see James Parks Morton saying it now.

That afternoon I wandered free in Central Park, and in the section of it called Strawberry Fields, in black-and-white mosaic in the middle of the path, it says IMAGINE. Imagine, and it can happen. A woman pushes a lady in a wheelchair up to the mosaic and lays a small bunch of roses on the word. The caregiver strokes the lady's hair. The birds are louder than the traffic here. People are quiet in Strawberry Fields; they sit on the benches and gaze at the word, or walk slowly round it as if circumambulating an altar. I walked round it and on till I came to a lake where a man was playing a silver flute with a hat at his feet. On down a path I found the boathouse café and sat there facing the lake, where three people in a boat were laughing with heads thrown back, the sun flashing along an oar, bouncing off the water, and throwing ripples of shade across the white awning above my head. This is New York? I wondered.

That evening I was sitting in another gridlock in Harlem on my way to the South Bronx. Marc Greenberg was driving. Marc had been running a successful family business until, some years before, he had walked into Saint John the Divine and been inspired by the sense of community there and the vision of the outreach programs. He offered his time, and before long he had left his business and was heading up a new initiative with homeless people. We finally came to a halt in a side street outside a building with a thick iron shutter over the door. This was the entrance to Project Success, a program in self-esteem and life skills that Marc had begun for people in halfway houses. Groups of men were lounging on the street corner. We made our way through a posse of crack dealers——none older than fourteen——to get to the shuttered door. This evening's topic was values.

"The most spiritual thing I know is listening to people telling their stories," Marc said as we began setting up the room, which served as a nursery during the day. "You just wouldn't believe the guts of some of these women—it's mostly single mothers who come to this program, and the hope and faith they have is an inspiration to me. One of them has five children by her father and her uncle. She was fed alcohol as a baby to keep her from crying. Yet she's coming through; she just knows there is a way for her life to make sense; she knows she has a contribution to make."

The room gradually filled until there were a dozen women and a couple of men sitting in a circle. A sixteen-year-old mother opened the evening with a prayer that was read every week. ("We're not especially Christian here, or even religious in the conventional sense," Marc had told me, "but we do recognize the presence of a higher power in our lives.") Another girl began by saying that despite all the trauma of her childhood, she had gathered some positive values from her parents.

"They were the ones who stood by me when I gave birth to my dead baby. They helped me through that, they showed me kindness then, and I try and remember that now when other people ask me for help."

"You're always there for me," the sixteen-year-old said, putting an arm round her friend.

"Yeah, we look out for each other, don't we?" her friend said and laughed.

"You know," said a large woman opposite them, "I want to say I really value this group. I remember how I used to peer in the window like the dealers outside and wonder what was going on here. It hit me that I was one of them a couple of months ago, out there on the street."

For the next couple of hours we spoke about our lives. One of the men said he had just been called for a job interview, and everyone clapped. A woman told how she and two of her friends were starting a computer literacy course. Then the woman who sat next to Marc began to tell her story. Her father was a murder victim and she had left home in the South, only to find herself living rough on the streets of New York. She became a cocaine addict and began selling herself to pay for her habit. Every Sunday she would sit on the steps of a church to beg. Every week the same family would walk by and the father would say, "You deserve better than this."

"One Sunday, suddenly, I got that from the inside. I deserve better than this, I said to myself. I got up and went to the hospital to sign up for a seven-day detox program. But I had no I.D. and no address, so they said they couldn't take me. What I did was I just sat there on a bench in the hospital entrance. I'm not going anywhere till they put me on that program, I said. The nurses would come by and give me food. Finally, after a month, they got around the paperwork and took me in. It wasn't enough, though. I was scared I would go back as soon as I hit the street, so I persuaded them to sign me up for the full forty-two-day detox. After that I got some halfway housing like you people have now, though the house was run by a Christian order and their condition was you had to go to church every day. I tell you that discipline saved me. Just the discipline of doing that every day. Anyway, I was on those church steps five years ago. Now I own my own house, have a college degree, and run programs like this one."

"Imagine the resolve these people need to climb out of the hole," Marc said as we hauled the shutter back over the door at the end of the evening. "Rosa—the one who runs programs of her own now—she's unusual, of course, but not unique. What this work is showing me is that somewhere in the depths of despair, if you go down far enough, you can find an incredible source of strength and faith. The human spirit amazes me," he added as we passed among the crack dealers and got into his car.

That night I lay awake listening to the sounds of the city, the sirens, the drumbeat from someone's radio, the buses, their brakes going down the scale like an organ pipe. What a great human heart this city is, I thought; a bleeding, pumping, surprising heart.

The next day I was on the Upper West Side, somewhere in the lower eighties, looking for the office of Rolando Matalan. "Don't think the vision of a global spirituality is ours alone," James Parks Morton had said. "People all over this city are dedicated to going beyond traditional boundaries. Take Bernie Glassman, a New York Jew and abbot of a thriving Zen community. They have started all kinds of projects up there in Yonkers, in the model of the Jewish ideal of spiritual practice in the marketplace. And Rolando Matalan, a young rabbi of a conservative congregation—he's quite special. You should meet him."

When I finally reached him, Rolando was busy, very busy. He and his staff were making the final arrangements for a street dinner party and celebration that was to take place that evening. They were expecting a couple of thousand people. On the desk was a photograph of his mentor, Rabbi Marshall Meyer, who had first started the congregation and named Rolando his successor.

"Marshall taught me to be passionate about whatever I do," Rolando said. "He also taught me that the greatest commitment is to the sanctity of life, to the revelation of the holy in everything. To lift the world, after all, is a classic Hasidic teaching—to involve oneself with everything, with suffering, with poverty, exploitation, prejudice. There is no better place than New York to do that. And people are ready to respond here because in New York, perhaps more than anywhere, many people realize that you don't get happy through money, no matter how rich you are. Because this can be such an alienating environment, people long for community, for the feeling of caring and being cared for. That is at the heart of what we do here. In nineteen eighty-five we were just thirty-five families. Now, eleven years later, we are seventeen hundred."

Rolando's congregation has no synagogue of its own. They share a Christian church with a Methodist group, a congregation of Ethiopian Christians, and a group of gay Latino Christians. Each congregation brings its own portable symbols.

"In this time, and especially in this place—New York—it's imperative to develop a transreligious language," Rolando went on. "Tomorrow, for example, I am meeting with Muslim and Christian leaders to discuss our various perspectives on Christ. We just don't have time anymore for all the old conflicts and rigid beliefs that belong back in the dark ages. The way we see it here is, we are seekers. We do not have the final answer, and we probably never will. What matters is that we support each other, those of different faiths, to look beyond our dogmas towards what informs the essence of all religion. I'm glad you are going to Saint John's for Francis Day. Maybe I'll see you there."

It was hard for me to imagine that I was speaking to the rabbi of a conservative congregation. In New York, though, anything is possible, as I discovered later, back in Central Park by the lake. It was lunchtime, the sun shining almost warmly now. A couple of young men with hair down to their shoulders, one with his shirt off, were strumming guitars. One of them was singing. A couple of cops stopped to listen, or maybe to move them on. Then one of the officers asked the singer, "Hey, do you know any Dylan?"

"Yeah, you like Dylan? What do you want to hear?"

The officer took his hat off, put it on the low wall by the lake, and started yelling, 'There must be some kinda way outa here . . .'"

Laughing, the kids launched into their guitars and sang along with him. The other officer, hat firmly on his head, kept his official stance and looked stiffly over his shoulder as if to check that his superiors weren't in the vicinity.

"Hey, it's great you guys are here," the bare-chested guy said and smiled. "New York's a great place now, safest place to be. You guys are doing a great job. Not like some of the beaches; you can't walk there. That's not America, is it? Hey, you guys are cool, hip cops, but then you gotta be in New York, right?"

"Yeah. Hey, let's do 'The Watchtower.'"

"'All along the watchtower . . .'" The cop started up again, the boys joining in, everyone laughing, even the officer with the hat smiling a little at the corners of his mouth.

Two days later and Saint Francis Day already. I took a cab up to the cathedral, to find a queue snaking its way all down the sidewalk, a full two hours before the beginning of the service. Inside, the nave was already half full; music was playing. A giant angel on stilts with black hair all down his back, a crown on his head, in flowing white gown, was dispensing his blessings to all and sundry with a wonderfully camp wave of his arm. This huge sacred space (the largest cathedral in the world, they say), columns soaring out of sight, light pouring in through rose windows of purple and gold—this resonator of the spirit was tingling, all electricity and excitement.

A light show started in the apse, pinks and yellows playing over columns and choir stalls. White-clad dancers of all races with twirling banners came pouring down the nave, around the altar, up into the pulpit—everywhere, it seemed—while Paul Winter, his consort, and the choir tuned their instruments, cleared their throats, tried a few notes. Every seat was taken now, five thousand faces peering keenly ahead to the altar in the crossing. Hundreds of hamsters and birds in cages, dogs and pigs on leashes—there being thirty thousand pet pigs in America now, the man in the next seat tells me, owned mostly by people who are allergic to animal hair.

Then in strolls the dean in a cloak made for the occasion, a real technicolor dream coat of gold silk and animals embroidered all over. He shares a joke with the stilted angel, who nearly falls over while bending down, and then ushers a dozen Buddhist monks in black robes to their seats behind him. On one side of the dean is Swami Satchidananda, the Hindu sage, in saffron robes. On his other side is Spotted Eagle from Canada. Next to him is Rabbi Gelberman, the leader of the Interfaith Seminary and the New Synagogue. And there is the bishop of New York with an eagle feather tied to his crook.

Winter and his consort pour their notes into the nave, a black soloist begins her part, and the "Canticle to the Sun" soars up to the fan arches and over the heads of all the assembly. More dancers come pouring in from the back of the church; the lights in the apse spread on out down the aisles; a

smiling man in a white vestment waves a censer in every direction; frankincense lifts into the air.

The music pauses for Judy Collins, the singer, to read the lesson, and then for the dean to give his sermon, this being an Episcopalian affair after all. He tells us how poverty, communion, compassion, and joy are the message of Francis. Poverty, he says, means an attitude of openness, an availability that brings communion with others. This in its turn arouses compassion, and the result is joy. And compassion, he says, is for the whole of creation, for the animal and plant world as well as for humans. Every spiritual tradition has a reverence for animals, and here we are now, reviving it in a Christian context, and not just us, because all over the United States today people are celebrating creation in their own festivals of Saint Francis.

The dean comes to a close; the entire congregation stands for the peace prayer of Saint Francis: "Where there is hatred, let us sow love . . ." Paul Winter lifts his trumpet, and down the nave floats the sound of a timber wolf. Thousands form queues for Communion, *Agnus Dei* rises to the roof, the calls of harp seals and humpback whales drift in and out, incense wafts down from the crossing.

It is already more than my senses can handle when the great west doors swing open, the world falls silent, and down the nave walks a slow procession of all the animals, led by an elephant and then a camel, a couple of rams, a bullock, llamas, a priest with a python wrapped round him, a man carrying a honeycomb swarming with bees, a woman with an iguana round her neck, someone with a goldfish bowl, a crab, lizards, snakes, a cockatoo, every kind of tropical bird, falcons, eagles, followed by all the animals already in the church with their owners, all of them heading for the bishop, who bestows his blessing with a wave of his crook.

Finally, as the last dogs are led back to their places, the choir starts up the hymn of acclamation, five thousand people stand, raise their arms above their heads, and sing, with a joy that overwhelms me, "For the beauty of the earth, sing, oh sing today . . ."

In those last moments of acclamation, arms stretched out above my head, I was lifted out of myself, shaken free of all preconceptions into a communion of souls in praise of creation. That night, down in the subway, I saw an old woman with a battered suitcase wearing a golden cardboard crown. Divine New York, I thought.

Sahara: *The* Fruitful Void

"Come with me into the desert." There is something
much greater than human action: prayer; and it has a
power much stronger than the words of men: love. And I
went into the desert.

— CARLO CARRETTO

Creaky old stairs they were, the ones leading up to the priest's
flat; oak stained dark, lit at the top by a dim light seeping
through one of those frilly little lamp shades that were fashionable in the fifties. Sister Paula was leading the way. She was
the guest sister at Twymawr Convent in Wales. She pushed
back the door at the top of the stairs. The wan light of a February morning
filtered into the room through two windows and picked out the dust on the
faded carpet. One wall was lined with bookshelves; on a table in the corner
stood an electric kettle, a jar of instant coffee, and some tea bags. Along another wall, the one with the wooden crucifix nailed to it, was a single bed
covered with a pink flock bedspread.

"You are most welcome to use the library." Sister Paula beamed a ma-
tronly grin.

"Thank you; I have brought my own books."

Already too late to bite my tongue. She meant no harm. She was being a good guest sister. But I was wary, on my guard. This was the first Anglican establishment I had set foot in since my childhood. It was 1975, and I was thirty years old, but already the taste and feel of the place were evoking images from my youth: the obsequious local vicar, the social hierarchy, the self-conscious hymn singing, the drone of the sermon that no one listened to, the keeping up of appearances, the call of duty. All so painfully bereft of passion, spirit, and meaning. Not just anxiety but arrogance fueled my quick response. I rather thought I knew something about genuine spirituality now, having spent some years as a self-professed seeker; there could hardly be much for me of interest on those dusty bookshelves lined with fading tomes on saints and church history.

She backed out of the room and left me gazing over the convent lawn to the single oak tree at the far end. Under the tree several plain wooden crosses marked the remains of sisters who had lived and died here. Beside them, behind a low hedge, was a trailer, the home of the community's hermit. I had come here for a week because I wanted time for reflection at a period in my life when events were moving fast. The environment of a contemplative community seemed an ideal context, especially since I had been told I could follow my own schedule.

I had not accounted for the way a place can seep into the pores: the smell of the furniture, the view from the window, the bells, the frankincense that came floating up through the floor from the vestry below to announce each of the seven daily services. I had not bargained for what I would find when, on the second day, unable any longer to resist the lure of the frankincense, I found myself irrevocably drawn down to Compline, their last service of the day. The chapel was a high, narrow cave, lit that evening with candles along the pews. The chanting of the nuns, the presence they summoned, their quality of attention evoked an unusual beauty whose effect stayed with me as I walked back up the oak stairs after the service and sat in the chair facing the bookshelves.

The air in my room was sweet still from the censer below, a bird was scuffling somewhere in the eaves. I got up and surveyed the books lining the wall. Bernard of Clairvaux, Catherine of Siena, Meister Eckhart, Carlo Carretto, *The Anglican Church in the Nineteenth Century.* I took down Saint Catherine and opened the covers. *James Lovage, Trinity College,* it said. *1936.*

The words went round a small red crest in the middle of the yellowing title page. That night I spent in Siena. I followed Catherine, entranced, round the city streets as she tended victims of the plague, oblivious of her own safety; I marveled at her visions, at her furious faith that seemed to transform all adversity into an opportunity to praise her Beloved.

The next morning I took down an author I had never heard of before. Carlo Carretto, *Letters from the Desert,* a small paperback among the rows of stiff spines. In 1946 Carretto was president of Italian Catholic Youth Action; in 1948, with the direct support of the pope, he organized a rally of hundreds of thousands of young Catholics in Rome. A few years later, at the height of his political and religious authority, he left everything to become one of the Little Brothers of Jesus, a renunciate fraternity in the Sahara. His book paints the great space and silence, the way the desert returns man to essentials. Reading his *Letters,* I realized how I wanted that. A vision began to form in my mind. Two hours later, I had decided to go on my own journey to the Sahara.

My love of the desert, then, began in a Welsh convent. In the summer of that same year I was on my way to Algeria, fired by a dream. My plane touched down at Tamanrasset airstrip in darkness. "Tam" was a tiny settlement then, in southern Algeria, not so far from the border with Mali. I spent the couple of hours before dawn in the little passenger building, talking to a mountain of a man with a handlebar mustache who was on his way to Chad to hunt rhinoceros. As the rocks began to glimmer in the first light of dawn, I clambered into the Jeep that was to take us to town. We bumped down the track, and within a few moments the Sahara was unveiled to my staring eyes, a vast rolling moonscape of red rock and dust, streaked with the purple and yellow of the emerging day. The sun that was rising over the farthest crags was larger than any sun I had ever seen. As it lifted itself higher into the gaping sky, the rocks burned redder and stood in stark relief against the canvas of blue.

The flight from London to Algiers had taken us the same distance as the flight from Algiers to Tamanrasset. The second flight, though, was over nothing but desert. The Sahara accounts for a quarter of the entire continent of Africa and is widening its borders every year. Tam is hundreds of miles from anywhere, in the land of the Tuareg, a proud nomadic people who still fail to recognize the arbitrary national borders across their territory. In 1975,

Tam was a few streets of low houses, an old French caravanserai, and a fort—all constructed in adobe.

The Jeep stopped outside the fort. I passed through the gate in the red walls and stood for a moment contemplating a tombstone with the inscription:

LE VICOMTE DE FOUCAULD

FRÈRE CHARLES DE JÉSUS

MORT POUR LA FRANCE

This, the resting place of Foucauld, was the birthplace of the Little Brothers. Charles de Foucauld had died here from a stray shot fired by one of the locals he was trying to protect. He had built the fort in 1916 to shelter the local population from tribal raids.

An aristocrat, a graduate of the Saumur cavalry school, a dandy who loved the best cigars and flirtatious women, he was sent in 1880 as a lieutenant with the Fourth Hussars to Algeria. He excelled as a leader but was quietly sent back to France over an affair with a Frenchwoman. At the age of twenty-four, in favor again with his regiment, he went on a solo reconnaissance mission to Morocco, disguised as a traveling Jew. The first Christian to survive the arduous journey into the interior, he returned with notes for a book on the topography and the flora and fauna of Morocco, along with a deep respect for the all-pervading religiousness of the culture.

Back in the high society circles of Paris, his book on Morocco a great success, Foucauld the adventurer was questioning his life direction. It was then that he was introduced to a man whose presence and simplicity touched him deeply. Abbé Henri Huvelin told him that he had long since found the means to be happy.

"And what is that?" asked Foucauld.

"It is to be willing to forgo one's joys," replied the abbé.

Foucauld went to Huvelin in the confessional the next day. Leaning into the box, he whispered, "I have come to you for instruction."

"Kneel, and confess your sins," was the reply.

"I have not come for that. I have come for instruction."

"Kneel, and confess your sins."

Foucauld did so, pouring out the deeds and events of his whole life. He

took Communion and left the church that day with a mission to bear witness to the presence of God in the midst of human life. He became a priest and spent most of the rest of his life living in the Sahara and serving the poor there, fired by the persistent dream of founding a community similar to that of the early Desert Fathers.

Foucauld's story was an epic one, and he had a part to play in my own presence here now before his tombstone. He had inspired many people to live in utter simplicity and anonymity among the poorest people in the world. Indirectly, through one of his brothers, he had inspired me to come to this fierce and lonely place for my own reasons. I have my own dream to live out, and I felt gratitude for his part in it.

I was a couple of days in Tam before I managed to find a Tuareg guide who was willing to take me out into the desert and return for me three days later. I had never heard of a vision quest then, but that was what I was wanting to do. My dream was to be alone out there for a few days, far from all trace of humanity, and discover who it was that really inhabited this body. As familiar as my moods and my preoccupations were to me, I was aware at that time in my life that there was a depth to human existence about which I had only the vaguest notion.

We rode out just as the sun was rising and continued until early afternoon. We stopped only for Said to dismount and make his prostrations and pray, and once to let the camels nibble on a bush of thick leaves and thorns. For hours we crossed a plain strewn with rocks and gullies. Mountains, some as high as ten thousand feet, ringed the horizon. They were part of the Hoggar range, the most ancient rocks in the Sahara, the only land above water when (in the Paleozoic era) the Sahara had been a vast lake. This was not the land of rolling dunes that I had imagined. I knew that only twenty percent of the Sahara is occupied by dunes, while rocky plains account for half of the desert, but childhood images are tenacious. The plain was more desolate, more sobering, than the Sahara of my imagination; yet more vibrant, too, orange and red everywhere, with streaks of black-and-purple shadow.

When we passed by two slabs of rock that were leaning against each other to form an open-ended cave, Said dismounted and untied a goatskin of water from the camel's flank. This was it, then. Three days under two rocks in a sweltering plain. With a word of farewell and a faint smile of bemusement, Said rode off with our camels back along the ancient riverbed that we had been following for the previous hour. As I watched him go, it occurred to me that I had never before put myself so trustingly, or perhaps unthinkingly, into another person's hands.

He disappeared over a slight rise and I turned to contemplate my surroundings. No wind, no trace of movement, no sound; everything just where it had been for centuries, or so it seemed, illuminated by an unfiltered glare; yet the heat, muted by the altitude of a few thousand feet, was bearable, even in high summer. Gooseflesh ran along my arm. I laid my bedroll between the rocks, heard my breathing, felt the air pass an electricity through me. Never had I been so tangibly aware of my own existence. I wanted to sing out, but the immensity of space took all sound away from me. The rest of that day I sat beneath the rock in awe, with a sheer animal joy, not just at the world I had come to but at the marvel of my own living and breathing.

Within a day, it was all rather different. The drama and excitement of acting out a cherished dream had evaporated. No longer was I playing the lead in some movie. There I was alone in the midst of this desolate landscape,

awoken in the morning at the first glimmer of light by swarming hordes of buzzing flies, churning out the same ordinary thoughts as I did back in London. Their triviality, my own mundanity, stood out starkly in the unswerving stare of the desert sun. I found myself beginning to laugh, not in self-deprecation but in genuine amusement. I was no great ascetic, no latter-day Charles de Foucauld or Carlo Carretto. There was nobody special waiting to be revealed beneath my humdrum exterior, no reserved destiny or Damascus experience about to proclaim itself on the desert stage. No, beneath the ticktock of my hopes and fears, past and future, there was nothing much to speak of at all, simply a sense of clear and empty space, rather like the desert itself.

I soon discovered I was not the first to stay in the vicinity of these rocks. Halfway up the outside surface of my shelter, someone had etched a swirl of rings into the rock. On another rock, a few hundred yards away, there was the clear outline of a giraffe, with all the detail of its shading, and on another had been carved some cattle, with long horns gracefully intertwining as if they were in some kind of ritual dance. The presence of the ancient ones survives here still, even here, where no one passes now except for the occasional nomad and dreaming foreigner.

The Sahara is the greatest open-air museum in the world of prehistoric rock art. Where I stood was once a land of flowing rivers and tropical wildlife. Elephant and hippo used to roam this way; oak, olive, elm, and willow grew on the Hoggar Mountains. These etchings before me were the accomplishments of men who had lived here, perhaps under the very rocks that were sheltering me, some five thousand years ago. Lake Chad, far to the south, is the only large body of water left from a time when great rivers poured through the Sahara to feed dozens of lakes across North and West Africa. This desert, which seems as if it must have been here since the dawn of creation, is just a few thousand years old. A million years ago people known as the Pebble Culture lived throughout the Sahara; their sharpened stones, the first tools, can still be found on the desert floor.

At night, my back against the prehistoric network of rings, I would watch the stars, stars that I had never seen, a whole constellation—Andromeda—I had only ever heard the name of. How much easier it must be to travel the desert at night, with such a compass overhead, the cooler air easing the way, an undiluted purity feeding the mind.

On my last day alone I walked out far from my rock into the empty expanse. At one moment I stopped and looked back over the way I had come. I seemed to have walked no distance at all. There was a wind that day, and my footsteps had already been filled by the shifting sand. There was no evidence whatsoever of the effort I had made to come this far. Suddenly, there in the uncompromising light, I was stripped of all self-preoccupation and artifice. I became aware of the deep insignificance of the personal story that I had imagined to be my identity. I knew now with a quiet certainty that the events of my life and the interpretations I had given them would pass like those footsteps in the sand. Standing there, a speck on a vast canvas, I felt returned to proportion: true, authentic, and unashamedly small, without even a story to tell.

When Said appeared on the morning agreed, it felt so ordinary it was as if nothing had happened. And in a way, nothing had. Bobbing up and down on that camel to Tam, I felt profoundly at peace with the world and myself. No ecstasy, no revelation, just the sense of being at home. I asked Said to take me to the Little Brothers, and he dismounted outside a house indistinguish-able from any of the others in the tiny back street.

The door was opened by a Frenchman in overalls. Frère Michel ush-ered me into a small room where two or three other men were sitting on the wooden floor. They were about to eat their evening meal. White bowls were before them; they invited me to take one for myself from a small table and to join them. One of the men was a visitor from another community of Little Brothers, in Mali. The rest lived together in the house and worked in the town. Frère Michel, a Parisian in his mid-forties with a fine, chiseled face and clear blue eyes, was working as a mechanic. Another was a baker. Their life on the outside was like that of any other worker in the town, except they attended Mass daily and prayed together each evening.

The Little Brothers are not a contemplative community, or a mission-ary or a charitable one. Their inspiration is the figure of Christ in Nazareth, the incarnation of love in the midst of daily life. They are invisible. They run no schools or hospitals, give no alms, preach no sermons, wear no habit. They seek out the poorest, the most socially neglected communities in the world, take on their burdens alongside them, and live out their lives in the practice of seeing the other in themselves and in the all-embracing love of Christ. There are perhaps two thousand of them around the world.

We said little that evening in Tam; mostly there was just the clink of spoon against bowl. They asked me if I had been to Assakrem. I had never heard of the place. It was the highest mountain in the Hoggar, they told me, some two days' camel ride away. Charles de Foucauld had built a retreat hut there, and a small chapel. Two brothers lived there all year round.

"God speaks on Assakrem," said Frère Michel in a matter-of-fact way. "It is so removed from the world there that it is difficult not to hear what one needs to hear."

"Strip your prayers, simplify, de-intellectualize. Reach God not through understanding but through love." These were the first instructions that Carretto, newly arrived in the desert, had received from his novice mas-ter. The Little Brothers were in training to be people of no importance, what Zen Buddhists call "the man of no rank." I understood now why the desert was their church and why they sought out the loneliest mountain there for their place of retreat.

A few days later, returned to my everyday world, insulated by glass and concrete, by cities and streets and cars and planes, by ongoing relations with others, I found it not quite so easy to remember what was obvious in the desert: that all the bustle, the urges to action, the plans and projects, veil a deeper, more lasting stream. Easy to forget, too, that nature bears an awesome majesty, terrible and mighty, that her wild places reflect our own untamed and primal ground. All the homage, the prayers, the love songs, the devotions to nature that have been sung on the wind for millennia are almost beyond our hearing now. For our ancestors, the voice or the vision of God would strike into the heart with a bolt of lightning, surge out of the desert, or speak on a mountaintop far above the tame and peopled valleys.

The voice of spirit cries out now in the wilderness of cities, and increasing numbers of people are hearing it, yet whenever I return to nature's empty wilder-ground, I am given a new breath and vision that restores me to my essential humanity.

I returned to the desert several times since my first journey there, though never to Tam. Yet that first encounter has never left me. Down through the years, too, the name of Assakrem lingered on, symbol of something not quite finished there in that forgotten corner of the Sahara. I would wonder occasionally—on a bus journey, in the subway, walking down a busy street—what unusual attraction this Hoggar mountain had held for Charles de Foucauld and why, with all the spectacular country around them, the Little Brothers would speak of Assakrem in such reverential tones.

Finally, fifteen years later, in 1990, I returned to Tam to take my original journey on to what, in my imagination, had become its final stage. Journeys are like that; they start out as imaginings, generated from a word heard here or an image seen there, then they take on a vitality of their own that may bear fruit just once, or even several times in a life. They can mature in a day, sometimes over years; but when they are ripe, conditions often oblige and bring them to the light of day. This time I flew to Djanet, a couple of hundred miles to the east of Tam.

Djanet is a tiny outpost in the southeast corner of Algeria, far from any paved road; far, indeed, from anything and anywhere at all. I wanted to take the long route to Tam, so that I could absorb the variety of desert landscape. I hired a local Tuareg team, one of whom walked with me, the others following us each day in a Land Rover with provisions. For the first couple of days we walked in a huge canyon that split open a range of red cliffs that soared straight up from the desert floor. Birds circled overhead, and I saw the tracks of hare, snake, and rabbit. On a rock lay a lizard eighteen inches long, a streak of iridescent blue. Old tree trunks shot out shoots of new life among twisted dead branches, and seed pods as large as small coconuts hung open from thorny bushes with tiny flowers emphatic as eyebright.

Beyond the cliffs was an empty plain, eerie and littered with black stones, like the aftermath of some volcanic eruption. Then, in the distance, loomed a mountain plateau, the Tassili-n-Ajjer, which means "mountain of rivers." Deep ravines and gorges were cut into its side, witness to the water that had once poured from the mountain. Olive trees, figs, dates, lime, and elm once grew there in profusion. This massive table of rock is the home of tens of thousands of prehistoric rock paintings and engravings. They must have lived in a land of plenty, those early artists, among all the animals of the present-day African savanna.

To walk with Mohammed, the Tuareg, was like traveling with an antelope. He moved over the rock and the sand like air, his long *jelaba* flowing gracefully behind him, his face covered in the traditional veil that protected him not only from the elements but from the danger of evil spirits entering him through the mouth or the nose. In the evenings, by the fire, he would tell me how his people had safeguarded the passage of caravans through the desert for centuries; how they were a noble warrior race who disdained mundane work; and how, more recently, the national governments had been moving them into settlements. He told me how they loved to eat couscous with grasshoppers, sand mice, and a big firefly called *dobb,* which according to him contained forty precious medicaments. One evening just before sunset we had stopped for the night when he pointed to a sticklike object standing up out of the sand a hundred yards away.

"That snake is very clever." He laughed. "He is standing up like that so a bird will come and rest on him, thinking he is a stick."

Traditionally, the only activities worthy of a Tuareg were war and raiding. When a family reached a water hole, the women would erect the tents, and slaves would tend the animals and fetch water. They would stay till the water or the pasture ran out, and then move on. Their policing of the caravans—of slaves, gold, and salt—was more in the character of a protection racket. Travelers had to pay to ensure a safe passage through their territories. The last great caravan, from the north down to Timbuktu, was in 1937; since

then the influence of the car has steadily eroded the Tuareg way of life. It takes 240 camels to carry the same load as one truck. The Tuareg are a mix of Berber, Libyan, and Greek blood, a unique culture with their own language, oral tradition, medieval tournaments and festivals. Some of them earn a living now guiding groups and individuals like me, though with the political troubles in Algiers, visitors are few and far between.

Mohammed and I wandered on past the Tassili to a pale yellow land beyond, where the horizon was broken only by sporadic outbursts of rock, dropped from nowhere and thrown together in untidy heaps. After a day of walking along an old riverbed, we passed across deepening sand through a forest of tall rock needles, to the largest dunes in the area. Nothing could have prepared me for this. The colors struck me in the chest; the desert floor was pale yellow, but then the dunes were bright orange, with a sudden shift in tone here and there the higher they rose. Occasionally there would be a neatly defined band of white between the tones of orange, and all of this against a sky so densely blue I felt I could plunge my arm into it. The shapes were designed by the wind: mountains of sand with twirling edges just like the soft ice cream that twists out of an ice cream machine, each dune with its own sharp crest that wound up to a point. The whole spectacle was unearthly, yet the Sahara takes up more of the earth than the whole of Europe. What, I found myself wondering, is more foreign to the earth: the desert, or the teeming cities of the world?

How simple it would be to disappear without a trace here. The Tuareg find their way by the stars and with the aid of signs—the color of the sand, the shape of a dune, a rock, a tuft of grass. In the early colonial days, two Tuareg guides drew a map of the whole southern Sahara for their French masters with bags of wet sand. One caravan that could have used that map set out for Timbuktu in 1805. Two thousand men and a thousand camels were never seen again. In 1933, Captain Lancaster tried to beat the flight record for London to the Cape. He reached Reggane, where he stopped for fuel, and the local French watched him take off. He was never heard of again. It was only in 1962 that his remains were found, by Titus Polidari, on a mission seventy kilometers west of Reggane. Lancaster had made a forced landing and had survived eight days waiting for help. His journal of those days, less the binding, which he had ripped off to make a fire, was tied to the fuselage. On the eighth day he wrote, "No wind. Dawn is breaking on the eighth day. It is still cool. I have no more water. I am waiting patiently. Please come soon . . . I had a fever last night."

On my last day before driving on to Tamanrasset we walked in the Tenere, another world to the land of the dunes. We had spent the previous night in the lee of a red rock, the last of several we had passed the previous day. When I awoke, I stared out from the shore of the cliff onto an endless sea of sand that was utterly becalmed; not a ripple, not a rock, no relief of any kind to break the mirrorlike surface.

After a few hours of walking on that plain I was jolted with the same realization I had had all those years before when I had walked out from my rock in the Hoggar Mountains: it was obvious I was going nowhere. This land was so much vaster than my stride that any idea I may have had of getting somewhere seemed ridiculous. Having no reference points also obliged my attention to stay where I was, with this step and then that step. I realized on the Tenere how our sense of self is so intricately dependent on the other, even if the other is no more than a contour in the land. Without even a contour for reference, Roger Housden himself seemed to slip away for a while, leaving little but the sensation of being alive—not as this identity or that, just aliveness itself.

We arrived in Tamanrasset in the early evening, and it was light enough to see that the town had undergone a transformation since I had last been there. There were avenues on the outskirts, a large army base, streets of concrete buildings. Tam was now the main administrative center for southern Algeria, and the population had grown from five thousand in 1975 to almost sixty thousand in 1990, including many refugees from the various troubled countries farther south. The old town was as I remembered it, however, and I checked into the colonial caravanserai with the cell-like adobe rooms.

Despite its expansion, Tam was still a slow southern town with an easy pace. In the morning I strolled out to the little square and sat with a coffee, watching the world go by. Not much went by—a few Tuareg, an Arab keen to change money, a boy who would have liked to sell me a Tuareg dagger, a man selling oranges. But everyone had a word to say, the selling seeming more of an excuse to gossip. Then a European woman, in her early sixties perhaps, with a warm open face and clear blue eyes, came out of a shop and made to get on her bicycle. I asked her if she knew where I could find the Little Brothers. "Will a Little Sister do?" she replied in French.

She came over and joined me. Her name was Sister Madeleine, and she had first come to the Sahara in 1959 as a nursery teacher. She had met the Little Sisters in Tam at Easter of that year, had joined them, and had been in different communities in the desert ever since. After the Second Vatican Council, they stopped wearing the habit and dropped much of the rule, living instead more from the inspiration of Foucauld, a simple life of being with others in the ordinary world. Even so, they still spent two hours daily in solitary prayer and an hour in "adoration" together. Sister Madeleine lived with one other sister in some rooms near their church.

That evening I went to their church to join them for Mass. It was a tiny adobe building with a sand floor, empty except for a square stone block that served as an altar, and lit by a narrow shaft of light from one small window. Outside was a small courtyard with an acacia tree and a well. Three sisters and four brothers came to the service, and two Africans. One of the brothers was Michel, whom I had first seen all those years ago. His features as clear as ever, he was graying now, as I was myself.

That church was like a desert cave, and it reminded me that I was in the Sahara again to restore my vision. I intended to go to Assakrem and stay there for a week on my own. Michel told me that a brother was going there in a couple of days and that he could arrange for me to share his Jeep.

The next day was a Sunday, and when I arrived at the church to speak to Sister Madeleine, thirty or so black men were listening to a man from Nigeria preaching in the courtyard. "Don't you know that God's foolishness is greater than man's wisdom?" he was crying out. "Didn't the walls of Jericho fall at the sound of a trumpet? Isn't that foolish? And you, you all want to leave Tam, you want to find your dreams in Europe, and it seems an impossible task. No money, no passport, no visa, and you want to go to Europe. Yet I tell you God will provide, and He will provide in a way that you will least expect. You must trust in His foolishness, brothers, and His foolishness will see you through."

It was an impassioned speech, and the longing eyes and cries of "Yes, yes!" from the congregation saddened me. I was being witness to a part of the world stage that I never knew existed.

"So many fine young men in search of a real life," sighed Madeleine as we sat on her step and looked on. "Thousands of them have poured into Tam in the last few years from all over Africa. They live in makeshift refugee camps on the edge of town. Their own countries—Zaire, Mali, Niger, Nigeria, Ghana—offer them nothing. The only option for them is to eke out a living on their family land, if they have any, and that is precarious in the extreme. Their countries are all on the verge of bankruptcy; there is often no higher education; AIDS is rife; the social structures are breaking down. The young don't want to follow the traditional ways of life anymore. Their eyes are fixed on the consumer society of the West. They imagine it to be a paradise there. They risk losing even the clothes they are wearing at the hands of Tuareg bandits on the border with Niger, and most of them arrive here with nothing at all. They cannot go forward up the road to Algiers, and they cannot go back, because there is nothing to go back to. The only ones with some money are the Nigerians, who have brought in the drug trade and sell their wives in prostitution."

How strange, I thought as I watched their faces; they dream of the West and I dream of the Sahara. Most people I know in Europe have money and all the consumer trappings, but they are in search of a real life just as these men are. I had come here, to the Sahara, because I, too, wanted to feel the real life that once again seemed to have slipped away from me.

That evening two Spaniards were eating dinner at the caravanserai. One, Abel, was a lecturer in fine arts at Madrid University. Every vacation he traveled to a different part of the Sahara photographing the prehistoric engravings and paintings. Back in Madrid, he digitalized the photos for posterity, with the intention of making the first complete record of all the Saharan art. He traveled everywhere on a 50 cc motorbike, using aeronautical water maps.

"I used to travel on a 500 cc Honda," he told us over coffee, "but I learned my lesson when I skidded and the machine fell on me. I was trapped for two days. I nearly died. I eventually managed to dig my way out, wearing my nails to the bone. 'When you don't know what to do,' my father used to tell me, 'find the animal in you.' I had to walk a hundred and twenty kilometers before finding help. Now I only take what I can repair myself. I drink two liters of water daily, and find much of my food on the way. There's no other choice. Most of these drawings are way off in the middle of nowhere. The Tuareg taught me how to hunt. I catch lizard, snakes, and hare. Snake is delicious if you cut a hand's breadth from each end. I catch hare using hooks and a circle of guitar string."

Juan was much quieter. A mechanic by trade, he loved to travel in the Sahara as soon as he had saved enough money. He wrote and published his own books of poetry. He was from Sorija, the town in northern Spain where Antonio Machado, one of the great Spanish poets of the twentieth century, had lived much of his life. Juan loved Machado and told me the whole town revered him as a saint. Every time he came to the desert, Juan brought toys that he would give away to the local children. The desert always attracts romantics, adventurers, those with their eyes on the stars.

As I crossed the courtyard on the way to my room that night I passed a man who was washing the dishes in a fat aluminum tub. He was singing his heart out. Our eyes met, and I stopped to exchange a word. He was from Zaire, he told me. He had left with his brother just before all exit visas were stopped. He had been studying biochemistry at university when all the schools and universities were closed by order of the president because they had been the scene of riots. They were still closed three years later, and the only people who could get jobs were those connected to the president's family. The president of Zaire, he told me, was one of the richest people in the world and had helped to fund the last campaign of President Bush. The people of Zaire were destitute, and he had come here in the hope of getting to Europe to find work and send money home.

"I know I will get there." He beamed. "I have so many dreams. I trust in God. He would not give me talent to waste in washing dishes. I know that so much is possible, but first I must earn the money to get to Italy. That is the easiest place to get to from Algiers. There are boats which will take you for a price, and the Italians, you know, they don't care so much about visas and all the official things."

Such life in his eyes, such hope in his voice. Our hands clasped, and we wished each other luck. I lay awake a long time that night, thinking of these African men, their dreams and longings like those of so many people around the world. It was fitting, somehow, that the desert, this empty and neutral land, should be the limbo where we all tussled with our devils and angels. Yet I felt an anguish for these men on the road in search of a life. Surely so much aspiration couldn't have grown merely to be whittled away here in the sand? I knew the answer to my own question, and that was what was keeping me awake. In the middle of the Sahara, where I least expected it, I was face to face with a global predicament. There is nowhere to hide now from the face of suffering. I wanted to help, run out into the yard and give him my money, but the worst thing was, I knew it wouldn't help: he would be back in the same situation a week or two later, when the money ran out. I myself was powerless to affect the situation. I had to stare the reality of it in the eye, and if my heart broke, so be it. This is our world, and I am as responsible for it as anyone else.

I met the Little Brother the next morning with bleary eyes. I clambered into his Jeep and we set off for the Hoggar along a track through the shanties on the outskirts of town. By late morning we were grinding our way up a narrow stone path that wound through gray cliffs and slopes of black scree. By the afternoon we had reached the rest house below Assakrem, a desolate stone building that served as a way station for travelers. With our provisions on our back, we started out along the footpath that looped up to the tabletop summit.

A low building with a courtyard came into view, just in the lee of the highest outcrop of rocks. A Little Brother appeared, greeted me quietly, and ushered me in to the courtyard to sign the visitors' book. "Your hut is across the top and on the other edge," he said. "There is a tank of water, but I hope you have brought everything else you need. There is one other retreatant here at the moment, a priest from Lille. But I don't expect you will bump into each other."

I thanked him and continued on up to the top. One square building faced the way we had come. It was the retreat hut that Charles de Foucauld had built all those years ago. A little way off was a small chapel, next to a tiny meteorological station that Foucauld had also built. The rest, a desolate expanse of black stones overlooking the most eerie and dramatic land I had ever seen. Off in the distance, across brown-and-black valleys, pillars of red rock rose up on the horizon: ridges twisted into sleeping giants; huge boulders strewn at random by the force of some ancient volcanic eruption; mountains in the shape of cones, saddlebacks, tabletops. Dust hung in the valley air below; an old riverbed snaked its way off to the east.

I followed the track that had been pointed out to me and came on a low hut on the far side of the tabletop. I stood on the plateau just above it, gazing at its walls of volcanic stone, its corrugated iron roof, its view over hundreds of miles, then made my way down into its little courtyard. The hut was divided into two parts, each with its own outside door: tiny living quarters, with a bed, a camping stove, a table; and a chapel that was bare except for a stone slab of an altar adorned with a miniature picture of Christ and an animal skin on the floor.

My head was feeling light already from the altitude; when the wind died for a moment, the only sound I could hear was the pulse in my ears. When have I ever felt so completely alone? Only when I was last here, somewhere down on that plain, fifteen years ago. I sat on the courtyard wall and gazed across the valley. Heavy clouds hung trails of vapor over the nearest crests, while on the horizon the mountain waves were shrouded in dust. I sat there till dusk and watched a crack of gold slit open the gray in the West. Two birds danced along the courtyard wall, then flew off into the void. A faint flurry of pink, and the day was done. The dun color of earth pervaded sky and land. I peered out over the fading view. "This is my religion," I said out loud. That night the wind rattled my cage from every quarter. The door creaked resolutely through the night, the iron roof flapped, two birds began

courting some time before dawn, mice scampered around beneath my bed. I awoke with a head thick from the altitude, a mouth furry from lack of water. I got up to wash, and there over the sink was a plaque with the words *Jesus, Master of the Impossible*.

Outside, a pale light filtered through clouds, the black stones and eerie peaks looking more somber than the day before. I was beginning to discover already that they wear you down, the wind, the rocks, the altitude. Try to think straight in a wind that whips through your coat from one direction, then stops suddenly, only to start up again from another side, and this at an altitude that has your head crashing before you are even awake in the morning. Nothing to look at but rocks for hours on end, volcanic ones with a magnetic field that turns the mind one notch away from its customary bearings. No green, no life, no relief from the burning ground. Nothing moves, nothing but thoughts in the head, and even those on a short lead that brings them quickly round to the beginning again. Meditation, which I had expected to practice regularly in such a perfect setting, proved to be more difficult than I had ever known.

That first day or two I held many conversations with myself; sometimes I talked to myself aloud. I surprised myself by noticing how I was already missing the bustle of town; I wondered about writing a novel to bring the plight of the Africans to public attention. What was I doing here, up here, "above it all," on some godforsaken mountain far from the world and its troubles? Everything came up from down below those first few days, the anger, the impatience, the torpor, the lack of direction or purpose, the lusting after voluptuous images.

For the first few days I stayed outside in the wind and the light, now up, now down, a slave to the buffets of mood and body. On the third afternoon I was sitting with my eyes on a small icon of Christ Pantocrator that was pinned to the wall of my cell. Suddenly I got up and, for the first time, opened the door of my chapel. It was dark in there, and the humidity soothed me. I sat on the animal skin on the floor. Something softened inside, let go.

Over the days that followed, my internal conversations began to give way to silence. To begin with, I had tried not to recognize my own boredom and depression; I had pushed them away with reading and writing. Now, as the days passed, there seemed less to be afraid of. Even when I was doing nothing, which was most of the time now, there was no sense of boredom to

run from. I had taken to sitting in the chapel darkness three or four times a day; just sitting there, the wind in the roof always. I see now why wind is the breath of life. Everything stirs in its presence; without it, this is a land of death, burned to cinders long ago by some prehistoric volcanic eruption. There was a taste of death on my own tongue, too. My house of cards seemed to be tumbling down.

In that chapel I began to see the sense, and also the beauty, in those old Christian terms "chastening," "being made straight." Like a bent piece of wood straightened with steam or an iron being made true in the fire. This mountain was knocking the stuffing out of me, returning me to an original mettle. The heart is opened, I was reminded again, by the awareness of one's own poverty. And what surprised me more than any of this was to find myself feeling a genuine sympathy for the Christian doctrine of original sin. Beneath all the perversions that have turned it into a weapon of oppression for almost two millennia, I could begin to grasp a deep and profound teaching that my own prejudice had blinded me to since childhood.

I knew on that mountain that my own nature—all human nature—contains a built-in fault line that severs me from authentic living. I had no choice but to see it—there was no healing balm, no soothing beauty to divert my attention. The beauty of the Hoggar was hard-edged; it reduced everything to essentials, to whitened bone. Another old word, I remembered, also much misused, was "repentance." The original Greek was *metanoia,* which means "change of mind." There was no blame or guilt attached to my fault line, but seeing it and accepting the fact were enough to turn the heart in another direction. By the end of that week on Assakrem, I was starting the day with an offering in the chapel. I offered my own divisions to that One—call it God, the Presence, the Self, the Beloved—who was more real, more true, than the contents of my own mind, and without whom I was nothing.

I came down the mountain in the company of the priest from Lille, whom I had not seen at all during the time I was there. I never saw anyone that week, except a shadow once on the rocks in my courtyard, whose origins I never discovered. The priest had been up there for forty days and looked like he had just come back from a weekend picnic, all jolly and jovial, and keen to find some fresh toothpaste. He was between lives, having been a school chaplain in Lille for ten years and now about to spend a year in America.

The first person I met on my return to Tam was Juan. He was sitting in the garden of the caravanserai, reading his beloved Machado. He read me one in Spanish, which I barely grasped the meaning of, and then asked me about my time on Assakrem. In answer to his question, I remembered an English translation of a verse of Machado that had meant a lot to me once. "This is how it was," I said. And I recited the lines:

> *I thought the fire was out*
> *I stirred the ashes*
> *And I burnt my fingers.*

In the morning, before leaving, I saw the washer boy from Zaire again. "Will you please do me one favor?" he asked. "My cousin left Zaire at the same time as me, and he managed to get to England. I know he goes to the church of the Jehovah Witnesses in a place called Wembley, near London. I have heard that through my family. He has been there two years already. Please will you find him and tell him I am here, at this address? I know he will help me. He will be so glad to hear from me. His name is Emmanuel."

I promised to do what I could. The following Sunday, back in London, I drove up to Wembley to find the church of the Jehovah's Witnesses. I got there early, before the morning service, and told the man at the door whom I was looking for. "He comes most Sundays," said the warden. "If you sit in this room I will bring him to you when he arrives." After half an hour the service was about to begin, and no one had come to the room. I got up and stood by the glass door at the back of the congregation. The singing had just begun when a man in a brown suit hurried in. The warden whispered in his ear and pointed in my direction. We went outside and I introduced myself, telling him about my encounter with his cousin.

He was dumbfounded, more uneasy than happy. "I am glad he is safe, but what am I to do? I am a mechanic here. I earn just enough to live in one room, and I am not even sure they will let me stay. My visa is only temporary, and I'm trying to do everything right to get a permanent one."

"Here is his address and phone number," I answered. "At least get in touch with him."

"But what can I do?"

"I don't know what you can do. I don't know what anyone can do. I'm here to give you the message. Perhaps the only thing we can both do is to hold him in our heart. Take him with you into the church. But here is his address."

The cousin took the piece of paper with the name of the caravanserai on it and folded it away in his pocket. We shook hands, he went into the church, I went outside. I stood there for a moment in the gray London street and breathed in a deep breath of dank morning air; then I saw the washer boy from Zaire in his hotel courtyard, whistling under a desert sun.

The Ganges and the City of Light

What is muttering, what austerity, what vows and worship,
To him in whose heart there is another love?

— THE BIJAK OF KABIR

I t was in my fiftieth year to heaven that I trudged along the path to Gaumukh, "the mouth of the cow." From out of the cow's mouth the source of the Ganges pours, next to a glacier some fifteen thousand feet up in the mountains. A sadhu lives there all the year round without a stitch of clothing. It was October when I reached him, and the pilgrim traffic was quiet. I had walked the narrow path from Gangotri, the nearest village, aided at times by the wooden rail that follows the cliff above the stream. The terrain is stark and rocky, with snow-covered peaks looming above on either side. I was cold and hungry, and my head was spinning with altitude sickness. I smiled wanly. He looked at me as if he had seen it all before a thousand times. His matted hair fell below his shoulders. A tiny rag was thrown across his thighs. "Which country?" he asked.

"England."

He nodded.

I sat there a few moments longer, trying to feel the sanctity of this source of all mercy and compassion. God knows I needed it, but it was not forthcoming in a way that my senses could register. I sat there an hour with the sadhu, aware, through a haze, of the austere grandeur not only of the mountains but also of him; aware also that some hours of stiff walking still lay between me and Gangotri if I was to return there by nightfall. Many pilgrims camp at Gaumukh, and still higher up at a spot called Tapovan, but altitude affects me more than most, and the walk down to Gangotri held out more relief at the end than a night with the sadhu.

I had just completed ten years of running a conference program in London on psychology, philosophy, and spiritual traditions. For some time now I had felt the need to step out of my roles, float free of the known, let voices speak in me that had been reduced to whispers over the years. At fifty, I was needing to return to essentials and let the world take care of itself. I wanted free fall, a gap. For that kind of space, there is nowhere like India. You want free fall? India has no floor and no ceiling. It can be worse than your worst nightmare and better than your wildest dreams.

I had first gone to India ten years before, on a journey of gratitude. In the sixties and seventies, when most of my friends were on the India trail, I had made something of a stand about exploring my own spiritual roots. Yet even then, India, through its sacred literature and biographies of its living saints, was lodged firmly in my imagined world. Two saints in particular, Anandamayi Ma and Neemkaroli Baba, kept appearing in my mind's eye, and though they had died some years before, I had wanted to honor what their lives had meant to me by making a pilgrimage to their ashrams.

I ended that first journey lying on a concrete floor for two weeks in the ashram of Satya Sai Baba, barely able to crawl to the toilet, hallucinating, vomiting, writhing in agony from stomach cramps. Just one of the initiations that Mother India makes freely available. I didn't think I would be going to India again, but as it happened I went every year of my forties, though never for longer than a few weeks at a time. Like most Westerners, I loved and hated it, the chaos, the noise, the squalor, the numbing indifference; and then the eternal rhythms and patterns of life, the grace of a woman carrying water from the well, the joy and vitality in the midst of poverty, the sublime spiritual teachings that still shine through the lives of certain individuals. I have never been so angry and so at peace as I have been in India.

It was heaven, indeed, finally to see the lights of Gangotri in the gathering dusk, and to slump for a few moments on the wooden bridge that spanned the rushing stream. Even I, with my splitting head, had to pause for a moment to wonder at these pink-and-white boulders at the foot of the ravine, sculpted with the ages by the river's persistence into living shapes that inspire many a pilgrim who passes this way. James Fraser, the first foreigner to see Gangotri, on his journey there in 1815, immediately set to work with his brushes and easel. By 1820, his watercolors of the Gangotri ravine were already selling in London.

Bells were chiming now in the temple to the river goddess, calling devotees to the evening *puja*. Not this devotee, though. I could think of nothing but sleep, and I saw no more of Gangotri that night than the door to my room.

In the morning I headed off downstream, feeling lighter by the minute as the way fell in altitude. I was following paths down the Ganges that wound through forests of cedar and pine from one tiny hill settlement to the next. In India for several months this time, I had started the journey of my fiftieth year with the aim of following the course of the Ganges on foot, by boat, and by train from its headwater, in the Himalayas, to Benares (which the Indians themselves call Varanasi)—half the length of the river. I had last seen the Ganges some years before, at Haridwar. Chloe, my partner, and I had rented a room in the tourist bungalow. One day we were sitting watching the river through the open door. The cleaner emerged from along the corridor and crept into our room with his brown reed brush. He was stooped, older than his years, a sad little man. I was prompted to ask if he had a family. "Yes," he said, and then, after a pause, "but wife sick, and children too. No money for medicines, very difficult." He made to start his work and then, as if remembering something, he turned and pointed through the door to the river. "But Ma Ganga will take care of us." Without another word, he began sweeping the floor.

I had never heard anyone speak of a river in that way before. For this man, the Ganges was a living presence, a protector, a healer of ills. And the sweeper was not alone: the Ganges is as alive as ever with the hopes and dreams of an entire culture. Even Nehru, that archmodernist, asked that his ashes be cast into the Ganga at Allahabad. For him, too, the river was India, more than any political party or ideal could ever hope to be. The whole Hindu world still comes to its banks to sing, to pray, to wash, to ask favors and blessings, to urinate, to barter, to die.

The Ganges is great not because of its size (it is fifteen hundred miles long, but there are many longer and wider rivers) but because, more than any other river on earth, it is a living symbol of an ancient culture's way of life and of the sacred dimension of nature itself. Of all Hindu goddesses, Ma Ganga is the only one without a shadow. She is the unequivocal fountain of mercy and compassion, here in this world only to comfort her children. Her waters are the milk, the nectar, of immortality, source of all life and abundance. Imagine the consolation that flows from her tangible, physical presence, a living emanation of the divine in this difficult world. No wonder that countless flowers are strewn across her body daily, that millions of lights set sail every evening upon her waters. While stories of gods and goddesses come and go with the ages, while one myth replaces or rivals another, the organic presence of Ganga continues as ever, absorbing her devotees' offerings and ashes in the same way she has done since time immemorial.

Ever since our encounter with the sweeper, I had dreamed of following the ancient pilgrimage route to the source of the Ganges and back downstream. Now that life had opened the way, I was following the first hundred miles or so from the source on foot. The walking, as always, threw me into a rhythm that my body and mind were thankful for. It aligned me with the motion of animals, with the occasional mule or goat that passed me at times on the way. It allowed for conversation in sign language with strangers, for a shared pot of tea with some herders. I could dawdle and watch the birds with tails a foot long, iridescent blue, flutter clumsily, on wings too small for their bodies, back and forth across the river. And always I could hear the persistent rush of wild water through the mountain gorges, see its turbulent white tufts, its fierce eddies and whirlpools.

My first day's walk from Gangotri ended with good fortune. As dusk was gathering, I reached a few houses clinging to the hillside around a hot spring that fell into a large pool. Within minutes I was up to my neck in hot, sulfurous water, the sores on my feet already a memory. A woman appeared, clothed from head to foot in bright red. She began circling the pool, making what seemed to be brazen eyes at me. She kept waving two fingers in the air and pointing to a hut farther up the hill above the pool. My imagination be-

gan to take off on its own. Incredulous, I got out of the pool and followed her up to the hut.

Then it began to dawn on me: the hut was a local temple, built on the reputation of the pool below. The pool was fed by two streams, one hot and one cold, which shot out of the hillside right next to each other. What clearer sign could you have of the presence of Shiva and Shakti, the male and female deities? The gods had blessed this piece of hillside, and the local *pujari* was there to make the most of it. The woman was his wife, and she was leading me up to the makeshift temple so I could leave some baksheesh in the offering plate by the door.

The pool, I discovered later, was a favorite stop for the Indian tourists and pilgrims who flocked through here in the summer on their way to Gangotri. The priest, it emerged, was the richest man in the whole valley, the only one in town to own a television set. Every dip in the pool is met with his or his wife's ingratiating smile and a finger pointing to the humble home of the gods in the hut above.

What struck me as much as anything else in Ganganani—that was the name of the village round the pool—was how quickly my imagination had decided the woman was making a sexual suggestion. Here I was, barely a few days out of England and away from my loving partner of ten years, and I was following a Hindu priest's wife up a Himalayan hillside, led on by fantasies of wild lovemaking with some anonymous seductress. Only afterward—I guess it's always only afterward—did I ponder the implications. On parting, Chloe and I had agreed the timing was perfect. For all the love and delight we shared, for all the pain that our separation brought with it, we knew that we both needed a space from our relationship to follow our individual dreams. We agreed that we would each be open to whatever arose during these months apart. What would I have done if my fantasies had turned out to be real? The idea was attractive, but I was aware of being seduced more by my own fantasy than by the actual prospect. There seemed to be something about this monogamy business—even at a distance—that went far deeper than mere rules of convention.

Just the one night did I take pleasure in the waters of Shiva and Shakti, and the next day I tramped on down along the riverbank, avoiding the road that snaked through the mountains a few hundred yards above me. Improbable corners of the cliffs had been cleared and terraced into fields of hay, gathered now into little stacks that dotted the hillsides. A government forester, surprised to meet someone walking his paths, told me to watch for the cobras and the mountain lion, but I never saw anything more wild than the bluebirds.

A few days farther downstream, I awoke on a ledge of turf by the water to see, here and there at the water's edge, a rock turned on its end and crowned with flowers. A man stood facing the rising sun, still dripping ice-cold water after his immersion in the stream, eyes closed and palms together in traditional greeting. He murmured some prayers under his breath, then turned in a circle on the spot, bowing to the four directions and letting a trickle of water fall back into the river from a brass pot he held out before him. He placed two marigold heads on an upright stone, lit a cone of incense between them, and with a final bow to the flowers and the river, he went on his way. To his tailor's shop, perhaps, or to his field. No fuss; not even a hint of self-consciousness at the presence of some open-mouthed foreigner. This was his way of starting the day, every day of his life, as it was for millions of other Hindus who honor the sacredness of the living waters.

Some days later, my mind and lungs clear of old air and already a joy rising, I came down from the hills to Rishikesh, the first town the river passes on leaving the mountains. I camped on a white spur of sand just upstream from the town. The river that had tumbled through canyons and ravines up in the mountains was wider, slower here; half tamed already, with the features of a civilization shaping her banks. The straw huts of orange-robed renunciates line the river edge; large ashrams and temples dominate the town. People are bathing, doing their laundry, praying, casting flowers on the water, selling pots. Bright swathes of color fill my eye: fine turbans, yards of cloth, blue and yellow, trailing from a woman's shoulder. Eternal gestures: the languid folding of saris, the passing of money, the feeding of children, begging, always the begging, and the placing of the sacred mark on the brow. The grace, wholly unself-conscious, of a woman stooping to place an offering, a leaf boat of flowers, into the water. Everything just as it has always been.

Walking along the bank one day, I passed a group of sannyasis in their orange robes chanting over an armchair in which an old woman was sitting. Someone was beating a drum, and a boat was tying up alongside. As I drew closer, I realized the old woman was dead. She was tied to the chair, still

in her renunciate robes. Next to her was a large box. Chanting continuously, several sannyasis lifted the chair into the box and began placing stones around the old woman's feet. When they had added enough ballast, they nailed the lid down and with some heaving and shoving managed to haul the box onto the waiting boat. The boatmen rowed out into midstream and unceremoniously tipped their cargo over the side. Sannyasis have no need of cremation, since their impurities are meant to be consumed while they are still alive, in the fire of their spiritual practice. Small children forgo the fire as well, since they are deemed too young to have accumulated bad karma.

Whenever I walked to town from my spur of sand I would pass the beach where I had met Mustaram Baba on my first journey to India, and I would pause there in gratitude for the way he had opened a door in my mind to let the inner teacher appear. He had been dead a few years now, but when I met him people would come from as far away as Nepal to sit on this beach by his feet. He was lying down by the water when I first arrived, all bone, sinew, and matted hair. A woman was massaging his feet. Someone else was feeding him fruit. He acknowledged my arrival by throwing me an apple——*prasad,* for the Hindus, or food blessed by the power of the guru. I had stayed there in the sand for an hour, and the *baba* never said a word. Words are of little use, I came to realize, for someone who can speak without them. The silence on that beach used to catch my thoughts like flypaper.

I had gone back the following day, and the one after that, just to sit there by the Ganga and let the silence soak in. I loved the casual informality of it all: no teaching, no ashram politics, no ritual, no ceremony. Mustaram Baba would just lie there and doodle in the sand with his forefinger; occasionally he would mutter something to an attendant about someone who was coming or who had just left. Nothing whatever seemed to be happening, though I was aware of a deepening communion between us that was being actively fostered by the absence of words.

After my last visit, I had returned to my room to meditate. As soon as I closed my eyes I was instantly aware of a seated figure in front of me. I was startled, because my meditations had always been formless; this form had arrived unbidden, and it wouldn't go away. I opened my eyes and closed them again. The figure was still there, seated in a relaxed lotus posture, apparently in *samadhi*. As I let my attention fall upon it, I was aware that the figure seemed to be shaping my own posture in the likeness of its own, drawing me up along the spine and holding me in a deep mood of gathered attention. I was being taught in some bodily way, "made good" somehow by a kind of magnetic force that was actively working on me in exchange for a simple willingness to be receptive. I never did speak to Mustaram, but I always "knew" that he had a part to play in the appearance of this figure. From that day on, this inner form stayed with me, for years. As soon as I thought of it, in any situation, its presence was there, far larger than my own.

One night I was jolted out of my sleep on the sandbank by a great rumbling and shaking of the earth. I scrambled out of my tent, but the world was still there. I had thought at first it was an avalanche, but there were no rocks to be seen. Only later did it dawn on me that I had been shaken out of my dreams by an earthquake. The next day I learned that fifteen hundred people had died in those few seconds, up in the mountains where I had been walking a few days before. *Ma Ganga, protect the forester, the priest and his wife, all those who gave me tea and hailed out a greeting. Ma Ganga, protect them all, bless them all, seen and unseen, in death or in life. Heal us all with your living waters that long to pour through our dried-up hearts.*

That earthquake broke the spell of Rishikesh for me and pushed me on another half hour downstream to the city of Haridwar, one of India's seven sacred cities. This is the place where Brahma greeted the celestial Ganga on her descent to earth; it is also where Vishnu (Hari) left his footprint, so another name for the place is Hariki-Pairi, "Hari's foot." The footprint is venerated in Gangadwara ("gate of the Ganges") temple on the right bank. Haridwar's waters are doubly sanctified, then, and 2 million pilgrims flock every year to this city of salvation. Criminals come here to disappear in the multitude of renunciates. Runaways from ill-fated marriages and family problems, bonded laborers on the run from tyrannical landlords, respectable families from Delhi, businessmen from the Punjab, villagers from Rajasthan—the whole world of northern India throngs in a mass along the riverbanks, all of them equal at the "gate of the Lord," Haridwar.

At dusk the river at Hariki-Pairi twinkles with a thousand lights. Leaf boats bob in the water with their cargo of flowers and a camphor flame, sent on their way by pilgrims anxious to secure the good favors of Ma Ganga. Bells chime across the city; priests are chanting down by the riverbank, waving their brass candelabra, ablaze with light, in the shape of the sacred syllable Aum. Pilgrims throng the Hariki-Pairi ghat, the most auspicious bathing place in the town, up to their waist in the sacred waters. The entire river, as befits a goddess, is garlanded with roses and chrysanthemums, their petals forming an undulating carpet across the waters.

I took a room in the same tourist bungalow that Chloe and I had stayed in a year or two earlier. Across the river, in the house opposite, we had met Poonjaji, a man we would never forget. Poonjaji was of the "already enlightened" school, whose supreme exponent is Ramana Maharshi. The school follows the advaitic philosophy of the Upanishads to its logical conclusion: If there is already nothing but the divine that exists, then what is there to achieve, and what path can you follow? You are already that which you seek. Seeking itself takes you away from who you already are. The only thing to be realized is that you are already where and who you need to be.

Such a path naturally excludes the concepts of guru, disciple, and a method to be followed. These presuppose ignorance and a path to be trodden toward freedom. For Poonja, there is nothing to be done: no meditation, no spiritual practice of any kind. All effort only takes you further away from whom you are looking for. At that time, Poonja did not accept disciples but was willing to engage with people in temporary encounters to help them see that they needed neither him nor anyone else to take them to where they wanted to be.

Our first encounter with Poonja had been in his tiny house in Lucknow. He was a handsome man in his eighties, with an air of great physical strength and nobility. There was no air of reverence in the room, no deep silence. It was an ordinary gathering of four or five people, assembled, it seemed, to pass the time of day. Poonja asked us what train we had taken and then gossiped casually for several minutes about the best and worst trains to Lucknow. Suddenly he turned to me and said, "What can I do for you?" There was a moment of confused silence before I said, "If there is only one undivided reality, Poonjaji, then how are we to account for the existence of love, since love requires a relationship?"

Poonja roared with laughter. "Now, who is asking the question?" he said. "Is it the question of a philosopher, or a lover? Either way, you are missing the point. Who are you? That is where you will find your answer. Tell me, Mr. Roger"—he insisted on calling me this from the moment I entered the room—"tell me, who is it that has come to India in the disguise of this body I see before me? If you can speak as that, you will know all about love."

"I suppose I can only say I don't know who I am. I am beyond my own thoughts and words. "

"But who is saying this to me at this very moment? What is the source of these words and this talk about love?"

I sat there in silence. I was tempted to leap up and clap my hands, like a practitioner in Zen might do when confronted with a koan by his master. It would have been a contrivance, and I sat there feeling uncomfortable under the gaze of everyone else in the room.

Poonja turned to Chloe and began to question her in a similar way. Then he asked the others if they had anything to say. When one of them spoke, he immediately turned their question or their statements back upon them. For a couple of hours this Socratic dialogue continued, until Poonja suddenly got up and said he would see us the next morning.

The next day, Poonja's questioning did push me beyond my own words. He was asking Chloe what she saw in front of her. She said she saw a yellow wall. "No!" Poonja roared. "The yellow wall was here yesterday. It is of the past, and only the eyes see the past. But what does the I, the Self, see?"

Then it hit me from the inside, and the words burst out of my mouth. "The I is not in time or space," I blurted out. "It is nowhere, everywhere. So the world disappears when 'I' emerges—because the I is the world. If the Self is the world, there is nothing to be seen because there is no separate seer. The Self can only see its Self everywhere. My God, now I see!" My body was alive with a sensation of aliveness, clarity, and a kind of joy.

"Ah, there you are!" Poonja exclaimed in delight. "Now, who is Mr. Roger now?" The whole room, including myself, collapsed in laughter.

Poonja had impressed us deeply, not because of any method or trait of character but because our way of seeing had been directly altered by his presence. Chloe, especially, had fallen into a depth of being that pervaded her ordinary life for months afterward. Yet we had taken him at his word and not looked upon him as a guru to whom we owed any allegiance other than gratitude. We had not seen him since our last trip to Haridwar, though I had heard that hundreds now gathered round him in a new ashram started by his followers in Lucknow. Since then, it seems, he has accepted the role of guru/father/divine being that hordes of hungry Westerners have wanted to cast him in. He now holds court before an adoring, weeping, giggling audience that is largely made up of the ex-disciples of Osho, or Rajneesh, as he was more commonly known.

I sat on the bank of the river outside the tourist bungalow, gazing across to the house where we had sat with him just a year or two before, so long ago now, it seemed. It was dusk; the bells were ringing downstream at Hariki-Pairi, the sky was streaked with purple and rose. The first question I had asked Poonja returned to my mind. I had glimpsed the one reality in which all things inhere; I could intuit the truth of *advaita,* that there is no such thing as you and I, only the one Self that we are. Yet since I had arrived in Rishikesh, an empty space had been growing in my heart. Whatever I did, wherever I went, the subliminal image of Chloe was in the background. However much I could acknowledge the ultimate truth, it was also true that I was missing her.

I was only a few days in Haridwar before I boarded the train for Allahabad, where I had an appointment. Another of the seven sacred cities, Allahabad in its turn is doubly holy due to its position at the confluence of the Yamuna and the Ganga. Geographical peculiarities add to the power of the land in India, and a confluence is especially holy, suggesting to the Hindu mind the image of the yoni, the vagina, the gate of all life. Allahabad is blessed with the confluence of not just two rivers, but three: the Sarasvati, an invisible underground stream, is said to flow into the Ganges at the same point as the Yamuna.

I was to meet up with a couple of friends in Allahabad. We intended to float downstream to Benares, fifty miles on down the road, and three days away by boat. We had a local agent arrange the boat for us, and early one morning he ushered us onto one of the small craft that lie in the shadow of the great fort. The skiff we stepped onto had nowhere to place the legs, nothing but bare boards to sit on, and scant cover from the sun. In the prow sat a shifty-looking, one-eyed character whose legs were thinner than my wrists.

He rowed a few languid strokes and then gave us to understand that we had to wait for his son. We were still waiting half an hour later. All the boats alongside us seemed sturdier than ours; they all had cushioned seats; and all the other boatmen seemed to be in the prime of their life instead of in the eclipse under which our own man seemed to be waning. When I made to leave for another boat, One Eye immediately discovered a hidden vigor and lurched us into midstream with the assurance that it was unnecessary to wait for his son after all.

His enthusiasm was short-lived. Other boats far more laden than ours, packed with fat pilgrims from Delhi or Bombay, sped past us toward the confluence, one of the most venerated spots along the whole length of the Ganges. At Allahabad, the river begins to take on the proportions of an epic waterway. At the confluence it has the appearance of a huge lake, with dozens of pilgrim boats moored there, out in midstream. Our boatman seemed to be taking on this formidable waterway with a nonchalance more fitting for an afternoon excursion rather than a trip that was to last three days. At this rate, we would be rowing long into the night.

Despite ourselves, we began to settle down to One Eye's pace, and soon all that could be heard was the creaking of oars (poles with bits of an orange box nailed on the end) and the distant chants and calls from a huddle of boats at the confluence, a mile or two from town. As we moved out into the main current, I noticed a figure walking in our direction across a curving sandbar on the far shore. The boatman edged us in the direction of the sandbar, and the figure walked through the shallow waters and out to our boat. It was the son. Everyone smiled; it was all preordained. It was only we who had been in the dark. In every small matter of life, and within the heart of all its chaos and confusion, India has her own inexorable logic, which the visitor can only learn to fall into. It is useless, utterly useless, to resist.

An hour later One Eye directed his son to veer off toward a small craft near the shore. For reasons best known to himself, he climbed aboard and helped the two young fishermen to clear their nets. Finally, he threw a few handfuls of sprats with large whiskers into our boat and we set off again.

We were almost the only other boat on the river. We saw one other fishing boat, and just a few dredges laden with sand, being hauled upstream by men on the towpath who were tied to the end of a long line attached to the mast. The sand had been scooped up from the central channel by buckets on the end of bamboo poles. There were no boats with engines. (The one outboard motor I saw on the whole journey was on the ferry at Rishikesh.) The only other craft we passed after Allahabad was a small wide-bottomed boat piled high with reeds. Among them, a flat, high-cheekboned face draped in white cloth peered out from over the steerage.

As we left the city behind, we wound our way into a landscape that could barely have changed in a thousand years. In dramatic contrast to the India that most people encounter, the river was silent except for the lap of water against boat and the cries of birds overhead. India has to be one of the noisiest lands on earth. Indians are entirely relational: they walk in groups, sit in bunches, travel in extended families. Their constant banter reaches a decibel level far beyond that of conversational speech in the West. They like to play loud music, of the Indian-film variety, to attract customers to their shops, to celebrate a festival, and to call devotees to the temples. The temple loudspeakers begin at 4 A.M. and leave no corner of a neighborhood unscathed. On the roads, day and night, Indian truck and bus drivers, who make up ninety percent of the traffic, keep their fists permanently on the horn, the volume and pitch of which is at the level of an air raid siren. It was a sanctuary, the river, an echo of what India must have been like fifty years before.

In the late morning, a band of vultures gathered on the left bank, taking turns at picking the remains from a blanched skeleton that had run aground on the sand. A little later, just before running aground too, One Eye surprised us with two words of English: "Dead body!" he exclaimed, pointing proudly into the water. The swollen corpse of a man, bottom up, still clothed, brushed by our starboard side. In the same instant, the son leapt out of the boat and waded to a collection of tall pots on the shore, where some men were stoking a fire. He returned with a pot of recently distilled rum, which, when we politely refused, he and his father set upon with relish.

Gradually our Western minds began to fall into the Asian rhythm. When we stopped a little later below a village fifty feet above us, we became entranced with the spectacle of a man up to his waist in the river washing his buffalo—rather than wondering where our boatman had disappeared to this time. In his absence the son covered a square piece of board with wet sand

and placed it in the middle of the boat. He smiled, and we smiled back. Some time later, the father returned with an armful of cow dung, which he set down on the board of wet sand. As we pushed off, he leaned over the side and filled a pot with river water. He lit the cow dung and placed the pot on the fire. When the water was boiling, he threw in the big-whiskered sprats and some yellow powder, smiling all the while, as if he were gradually letting us into a secret.

Bitter smoke began to blow in our faces. There was no escape from it, and I longed for their dinner to be over. We tried lying on the deck, we squirmed into a dozen different positions, but the smoke followed us everywhere. They, on the other hand, being upwind because that was where the oar sockets were, smiled beneficently all the while.

Fortunately, there was a current; if our progress had been left to the oars, we would still be on our way to Benares now. And yet drifting down this river was a wonderful thing. This, I remembered, was what drew me back to India time and again. A woman with a pot on her head swayed up steps that were etched in the mud; children played by the shore; a grandmother washed her linen; buffalo snorted in the river; vultures huddled on the sand. A stillness came over the river, the wind died, and dolphins, dozens of dolphins, wheeled and dived alongside us. Both riverbanks were of caked white sand, and ahead of us they merged into each other around great sweeping bends. We seemed to be on some vast, tranquil lake, floating through a land where time had been banished.

As the sun began to dip to the horizon, the boatmen took an oar each. They seemed unable, however, to row in rhythm, so that one soon fell behind, until the other caught him up again. An hour after dark we saw the flashing light of our agent, who had already set up camp on the bank. Two days later, through an early-evening haze, we glimpsed the outlines of the palaces and temples, all pink-and-brown, that line one of the most dreamlike riverfronts in the world. We were finally entering Shiva's city, Benares, where death is defeated. From the source to the City of Light I had come. I cupped my hand in the water, lifted it to the dying sun, and let it trickle back into the stream. I remembered the sweeper in Haridwar and knew the water to be on my own breath now.

City of Light, City of the Dead, the Forest of Bliss, the Never-

Forsaken, the City of Shiva—Benares, known locally by all these names, is unquestionably one of the maddest, holiest, ugliest, most entrancing cities on earth. From the river we all had the dreamlike sensation of floating in a boat through the city of the gods. The light falls on the temples, the palaces, the water with a radiance that is equaled nowhere. A man meditates by the shore; sadhus walk by with their staff and water pot; people squat, having their heads shaved. A woman bathes in the silky water; children play chase among the funeral pyres; somewhere, bells are ringing; a huddle of people, all in white, gaze on as the body of one of their relatives crackles and dissolves in the flames of a great fire.

As soon as we stepped ashore, however, having shaken hands with One Eye and his son (for whom by now we felt nothing but affection) and gathered our bags, the assault began. Every deformity imaginable is displayed in the queue of beggars lining the road to the main ghat; every trick in the book is routinely used by the touts, the rickshaw wallahs, the boatmen, the shop agents to part another fool from his money. My friends took off for the railway station and the night train to Calcutta. I walked along the ghats—the colossal flights of stone steps that lead down to the water's edge—to Assi, the southern limit of the town, to my favorite hotel on the river, quickly drawing a motley swarm of hangers-on like bees to a honeycomb. I intended staying some weeks in this, the heart of Hindu faith and chicanery.

The steps shone a burnished gold in the evening sun. On some of them, the washermen had laid out their day's work to dry: yards of sari, blue and bright yellow, stretched down toward the water. Here and there people were squatting watching the river go by; dogs ran between them, snapping at one another. Overhead, two vultures circled.

I knew I had arrived at Assi ghat when I saw the pipal tree by the shore. A barber sat next to it, ready to serve those on their way down to bathe. On their way back from the river, the bathers make straight for the pipal and circle it, placing flowers, rice, and a sprinkling of Ganga water on the holy images around the tree. They smear vermilion on its trunk, throw a few grains of rice at it, and put the same hand to their foreheads. Some stand for a few moments facing the tree, palms together, praying intently to their chosen deity. The pipal at Assi is as sacred as any temple. I settled into my room and later, when the river had gone quiet, went out to end that day back on the ghat, alone with a new moon rising through the branches of the sacred tree.

I had entered a sacred cosmos, a world where nature, humanity, and the stars are woven into a seamless piece. For Hindus, Benares is the embodiment of heaven on earth. Another name for this cosmos is India, for India was always conceived by its inhabitants to encompass the universe. So Benares is India, and there is in Benares an exact, scaled-down version of every major site in the country. The seven sacred rivers are all represented here by different streams; there are seven replicas in the city of the great temple of Rameswaram, in Tamil Nadu. All the twelve major lingas of India are

here, and so on. Benares is India—not just in some poetic or mystical sense, but in a tangible dimension of energy. Come here, say the scriptures, and you can forgo all other wanderings.

A few days later I met up with an old friend, Dr. Rana Singh, a lecturer at the Benares Hindu University. As we strolled through the lanes of Assi we passed a narrow doorway that opened onto a steep flight of steps leading down into the basement of a house. I peered in. Below me was a linga set in a marble surround, with men packed round it on all four sides chanting in unison. "The Jyotir-linga," Ranaji explained. "All the twelve Jyotir-lingas of

India—the lingas of light—are represented in Benares, but this one is the essence of all the twelve."

Whatever the official story, what I could see was a huddle of men down in the womb of Mother Earth, in semidarkness, paying homage to a phallic symbol. We climbed down to join them and squeezed into a corner of the tiny room. In minutes, the chanting had lulled my thoughts away. Occasionally, one of the men would pour rice over the linga. Another would light a camphor flame. The chanting grew to a pitch, a large conch shell was blown, and suddenly it was all over. Everyone stood and filed up the steps, leaving Ranaji and me in an empty room with a linga covered with rice. As we got up and slowly made our way to the daylight, I felt we were coming out of some burial chamber and we were the risen ones.

Later that evening, having wandered for much of the day in the company of Ranaji and enjoying his stories, I went back to sit on the ghats. One or two lamps were floating on the Ganga. Shrouded bodies lay snoring on the steps. Some Naga *babas*—the ones who go naked, covered in ashes— were sitting by the Ganga smoking a chillum of *bangh,* the local hashish. Someone was playing the tabla at one of the windows of an old palace. A group of twenty young men were chanting softly up on a step. I remarked to one of them how unusual it was to see people of their age singing devotional *bhajans.*

"We call ourselves the Vivekananda Club," he replied. "We are all in the Engineering Faculty at the university. Yes, it is very rare. We just feel there is more to life than films and career. We want to ask the deeper questions of life, and we feel our old traditions can help us, without having to join some traditional group."

I sat with the Vivekananda Club for a few minutes, filled with a new appreciation for engineers. Then, at the prompting of the mosquitoes—or so it seemed—I went back to end the day in my room. The neighbor's buffalo was lowing outside my window. I picked up my pen to write, sat there a few minutes in front of the blank paper, and suddenly, quite unexpectedly, burst into sobs. I sobbed and sobbed from somewhere deep, deep inside, and I didn't know why, or where it had come from, except some great longing, some far-off call, unnamable, seemed to be filling my body from head to toe. And in among my sobs and this great aching pain there rose somewhere the name of my loved one.

I woke in the morning feeling emptied, scaled down to size, my sharper corners rubbed down. The best word I know for it is the old Christian one "shriven," which pointed to the purpose of Lent. I was meeting Ranaji again that morning, though I had had my fill for the time being of lingas of light, temples, wells of wisdom, and sacred circuits. I needed rather to follow the course that seemed to be emerging in my own inner stream.

"There is a sadhu I would like you to meet," Ranaji said when he arrived. "He is an unusual man, a Gorakhnathi *baba*, one of the few genuine ones who eat only fruit and milk and generate the power of Shakti through breathing practices. Most Gorakhnathis sit by the roadside smoking their chillums, but people seem to agree that Devbarnath Yogi has reached the ultimate goal of *moksha*."

This was hardly an invitation to decline. We went off to meet the sadhu in one of the backstreets of the town. Devbarnath Yogi's joy struck me as soon as we entered the courtyard of the dilapidated Gorakhnath ashram. He was seventy-two and looked twenty years younger. Through Ranaji he told me that, some forty years before, he had once been a householder, and had married for love—a rare event in India, where most marriages are arranged by the families. Unfortunately, he had fallen for a woman whose family was wealthy, and from a higher caste. Her family made their lives so intolerable that eventually he left to become a sadhu. He heard later that his wife had died of a broken heart sometime afterward. They had had no children, and he continued his wanderings, eventually joining the Gorakhnathis. He practiced fanatically; many of his fellows thought he was mad, but in fact he was wild with grief. His pain gave him the energy for all his austerities, and eventually it was subsumed into an all-encompassing love. After some twenty years, he said, he finally attained full absorption into Shiva.

"You must let Shakti have her way with you." He laughed, looking at me closely. "When Shakti rises, the mind wants to run away from her." He paused for a second, leaning back and roaring with laughter. "But you must let her catch him. Keep the mind in front of her, so she can swallow it. Once the mind feels the electric current rising up the spine, it won't want to move. You will hear a tinkling sound in the body, too. Each of the energy channels up the spine has its own sound. When Shakti is activated, you will hear the conch, the drum, and the flute inside your body. On the other hand, perhaps you will hear nothing. It depends on the individual. But once Shakti is awakened, you will see no more distinctions of caste or creed, and you will know the past and the future. Thinking ill of others, saying ill of others, doing ill to others——these are what prevent Shakti from flowing. You will remove all these obstacles once you trust absolutely in the power of Shiva, the Lord."

If Shakti rises, I thought, I am all too ready to let her have her way with me. I don't really see what else there is for me to do. I thought these things, but I didn't say them to Devbarnath. I kept them in the cave of my heart, and Ranaji and I stooped through the low ashram entrance and back out into the sun. I stayed in my room for days after that, sitting there listening to the buffalo, staring into space, praying without words, wondering about home, boring myself, feeling nourished by the intimacy of interior silence.

The first place I went on leaving my room was to Manikarnika, the burning ghat, the portal of death and liberation. Half a dozen fires were burning near the water, and other corpses, trussed in yellow-and-gold cloth on bamboo stretchers, were waiting their turn nearby. The fires burn day and night, consuming bodies that are flown in from all over India, and even from places as far away as London, by relatives anxious to smooth the passage of their loved one to heaven with the most auspicious end conceivable, in the Ganga at Benares.

The family members were sitting above, watching the proceedings in silence. A wide-bottomed boat heaves to with another mountain of logs for the fires. An eldest son, head shaven, clothed from head to foot in a white robe, walks down to one of the fires that has done its work, throws a pot of Ganga water over his shoulder onto the embers, and without looking back rejoins his family. The last rite completed, they all troop off to bathe for a last time in the river.

I ambled along after them and began to head back to Assi. Just then, a procession of drummers and pipers came down to the water, leading a flower-covered bier, chanting, *"Ram, Ram, satya he!"*—the mantra that accompanies every corpse to the fire. Just before the fire they stopped, and two young men leapt out in front of the body, which was still on the shoulders of the bearers. To the encouragement of the beating drums, they threw themselves into a wild sexual dance, one with a stick in his trousers that seemed to give him a massive erection, the other gyrating his pelvis like a woman, his arms and forefingers prodding the air. Round and round each other they turned, entirely given over to what I could only assume to be some ancient evocation of fertility and new life. The musicians circled round them, drumming the dancers into an ecstatic frenzy. By now everyone was clapping and laughing, and as the dancers' exhaustion slowed them down, they motioned me to come and join them. I had never been to a funeral like this before. Perhaps it was that, perhaps it was something else, but I backed away, laughing and shaking my head. Just a few minutes later, too late, I wished I had danced that cremation dance.

Soon after that my last day in Benares dawned. I had already decided to spend the day walking the path of the Buddha to Sarnath, where he gave his first sermon. Within an hour or two I was leaving the city behind and making my way up and down paths that wound their way through woodland from one small village to the next. I had been aware on waking that a heaviness, by now quite familiar, was weighing on my chest. Even here, in this magical landscape, following the very paths that the Buddha had taken, I was heavy with the absence of my beloved. This time, I let myself feel without restriction the burden I was carrying. And suddenly it struck me: I was actually choosing to carry this weight around with me, like some kind of identity—the suffering lover. It was like walking round all day with a heavy stone in my rib cage, though it had become so familiar I had come to see it as normal.

In a flash I saw how I was doing this to myself, like some martyr. In that instant, all the leaves of the trees began to glisten with light; the air felt electric, the ground full of vibration. I saw beyond any doubt that the true goddess, the one true Beloved, was everywhere, in every living particle. The weight slipped from my body. I was filled with light, the leaves shot out colors like crystal prisms, and I was filled with the most unutterable joy. I opened my arms out wide and began turning, turning, like some mad dervish drunk with life. This dance was my own true dance, and I was dancing it now.

Big Sur
Dreaming

*You have only to let the place happen to you . . . the
loneliness, the silence, the poverty, the futility, indeed the
silliness of your life.*

— KATHLEEN NORRIS

On my way to New York a few months before, I had stood in line for the Heathrow security check behind a woman who was in a hurry. "Where are you going?" I asked her. "Sedona. You know it?"

"No, but I'll be taking a journey through the Southwest later in the year, and so many people have mentioned Sedona to me recently that it looks like I might just have to start there. Now here you are telling me you are on your way there."

"I've been living there for ten years. It used to be an incredible place. Too crowded now, though. I'm packing up and moving to Norway. My boyfriend and I have bought a boat there, and we are going to sail round the world. The oceans are the only great spaces left."

Perhaps, but meeting her was the final synchronous nudge. I would start my journey in Sedona. Red-rock, Hopi, Navajo land. The American fantasy, wild and free, exported to the global consumer courtesy of Harley-

Davidson and the Marlboro ads. All those clichés swirled up out of the desert dust to feed the dream of the hero riding into the sun. They are fuel not just for the Hollywood engine but for the collective dream of America, the immigrant's dream of a new life, a New World, a mad hope that persists even now in the face of mediocre politics and a fractured, dislocated society that manages to produce the fattest and the fittest people on earth. If those clichés have power it is because we are all heroes, we are all on an impossible journey, forging so seriously a life that we know will dissolve in a twinkling. And for a European, an Englishman especially, the size of the place—the big skyline, the unfenced rolls of plain, mountain, desert, the unmitigated blaze of the American Southwest—suggests a return to the undiluted natural world, to the animal in us, the wild.

At Heathrow again, I met a friend, sold him my car, and boarded a plane for Phoenix. What's in my baggage? A clean slate. Just a memory of red rock from a Greyhound journey I had taken down Route 66 back in 1965. An open mind. Clouds the color of indigo, a silver wing tip, barren islands off Scotland, white horses on the Atlantic, rivers of ice down in Greenland, and barely a scrap of agenda. No escape from anything, no great desire, no question. Just following the wind that blows me that way, a rare breeze for me to bend to.

The sun isn't shining in Phoenix. "Watch out for the winds," the car rental lady told me. "It's beautiful up there in Sedona, but there's a storm coming up."

Past Little Squaw Creek, Dead Man Wash, Horse Thief Basin, on through the desert to join the tail of a traffic crawl into Sedona. Crystal shops, tours round the energy vortices, Pink Jeep rides to Cathedral Rock and Bell Rock. In the grocery store three women trail around in purple velvet cloaks, a golden snake embroidered on each back, hoods over their heads. In the coffee shop a woman at the next table sits with arms spread wide and eyes closed as her male companion gives her spiritual advice.

The clouds gather heavily, but even so droves of tourists pour over the red rocks and into the trinket shops. They say the rocks tingle here, and I swear that big Bell Rock did just that when I crawled up its side, and I'm not given to imaginings that easily. But then later I thought that I too would tingle if I had as many people as Bell Rock does trampling over me daily.

The next morning a foot of snow has fallen in Flagstaff, just a few miles away and a couple of thousand feet higher than Sedona. I drive up to see Oak Creek Canyon hung with crystal and find a busful of Germans buying jewelry from an impassive Navajo. An acquaintance with the right connections has scheduled me to meet some of the Hopi elders, and then to stay in a Navajo hogan (their traditional native dwelling) up in Canyon de Chelly; except the road may not be clear, and maybe we should wait in Sedona a day or two and see what the weather does. I can feel my red rock dreams melting away. At three in the morning I awake with a start and I call out loud.

"Big Sur," I say, "that's where I'm going."

I don't know why Big Sur, except you don't argue with a command that comes out of your own mouth in the middle of the night. All I know is too many crystals wear thin on me; and snow——hey, I'm from the gray winterland. Who needs it to start this early? These aren't reasons, though; you just never know where a journey will take you when you follow the wind. So much for synchronicity and Sedona. With the light coming up over rocks veiled in fog, I head out west for a warmer land.

In an hour or less I'm up on the crest of a big ridge, parking my car in the town of Jerome, a ghost town revived, it looks like——timbered houses, half shut down and half artists' studios. I get out of my car and walk smack into John Dempsey, who owns the House of Joy. Anyone who owns a restaurant called the House of Joy has to be talked to, and John makes that easy. In fact he is talking to me before I've shut the car door, about how he's listed as one of the top one hundred restaurants in the United States, and not even a tablecloth. His sign is a gartered stocking, and he tells me that the very same place was once the biggest brothel in town (it being legal then), for back in the early fifties Jerome had seventeen thousand workers here mining for copper. He ushers me in and shows me the little cubicles that used to be the scene, I imagine, of a certain relief from the mine and are full now, each one of them with a pine table for two and a tall silver candlestick. On every available ledge and windowsill dolls are piled high; not ordinary dolls but ones with surprising and endearing expressions that John has made himself while his wife makes their clothes. So many ways to live a life, and John Dempsey is living his a happy man.

I thank John for his warm introduction to the little town, move on out over the mountains, with the country music high, to Prescott, and on through Salome past dozens of trailer parks with folks out to pasture, on over the border into California through Desert Center (a gas station and a grocery store), all the way at last to Santa Monica, where the great continent finally gives out and stops short in the spray of Pacific rollers. The beach here is an extension of the town. Everything in order; you keep to the walks and take a turn only when they do. In the late afternoon the light is silver, and the snow a fading memory from yesterday already. An old man shuffles by in a crumpled brown suit and cloth cap, stooped with his gaze on the sidewalk as if there may as yet be undetected traces of gold in the gutter. Santa Monica is not all glitterati, not what it seems.

I'm not even started yet. This is not the beach I'm looking for. I'm still on my way up the coast, drawn by a Big Sur reverie. The next morning I pull into Harmony, population eighteen, "Town for Sale." A few artists selling their pots and paraphernalia, and a coffee shop, closed. Down the hill is Cambria, a warm, comforting place, all half-timbered buildings with slate roofs, wooden verandas with Grandma Portes selling turkey sandwiches, and a barber's with an original red-and-white pole. I have a haircut, a spring clean, because this is the beginning of I don't know what. Just up there on the ridge, Big Sur, beginning at Ragged Point. The barber—he must have shorn the whole town in his time—tells me he has been on this corner for eighteen years, "And I'm glad as can be, because I tell you this is the most beautiful corner in the world. I came from Bakersfield; got to be one of the hottest places anywhere. I didn't want to die in a hot place. I told them, if I die here, take my body to the ocean and bury it there. But I got here before then, mercy be."

At Ragged Point the road rises to climb the first of the Big Sur cliffs that fall into the sea with no hint of apology. There, I met a master. The spiritual teacher Georgy Ivanovich Gurdjieff once said—and Gurdjieff would know—that if someone could show him a man who had mastered one thing well, he would show him a man who had forged a soul. On Ragged Point there is a master cappuccino maker. He has a booth by the gas station. He learned his art from an Italian in Colorado, and through his art shines an unmitigated love for what he does. He relishes in making coffee tailored for you; he delights in discovering your particular whims and fulfilling them to the last degree. Everyone likes their coffee different, especially now that you can have a *corto, macchiato, ristretto,* latte, depth charge, and add syrup of amaretto, vanilla, white chocolate. The master at Ragged Point leaps deftly to his silver machine and pulls the lever to squeeze out the black juice just in the measure you need but hadn't quite made conscious. While you are waiting he tells you what you are getting, where the coffee came from, and that the secret of all good cappuccinos is to look after your machine with daily cleaning. His specialty in Colorado, he tells me, was cappuccino with a shot of blueberry syrup and Bavarian chocolate blended into the foam.

I thank him for the coffee and his love of the art and climb over the bluffs round the bends of Highway 1 with the big ocean view filling my window and the steep rise of the Santa Lucia Range off on my right. For some reason unknown to me I am beginning to feel exposed on this journey, a small branch on a hill in a big wind. It can be a lonely road, Highway 1. Through Gorda I go, the gas station with a few cabins for rent, named after the big rock, "the fat one," off the shore; to Lucia finally, my first resting place here where a night voice drove me, Big Sur. On the ocean side of the road is a wooden shack of a restaurant with a gas pump outside. A few paces farther along some cabins hang precariously to the cliff edge. I barter with the owner, it being off season, and take the keys to number five. Over the bed the black ceiling rafter bears the name of an earlier guest, *Paul,* carved into the wood for perpetuity. The gulls shriek, the night falls.

On the ocean side of the Lucia restaurant a wooden veranda opens onto a Pacific spangled with silver and strands of mist that hug the base of cliffs plunging sheer into the placid waters, ramparts that daunted even the Spaniards. (They sailed on by to Monterey.) The Lucia veranda is one of the finer places in the world on which to have breakfast. In the mornings the bluffs are hung with a mystical light, pale blue and green. I sit there and take my time with eggs over easy and with the dawning realization that this is a sacred journey like no other I have taken. Now that I am here, I have no particular destination, no route to follow, no apparent challenge, physical or otherwise, no arduous trek to set out on, no sacred site or shrine to reach. This is it: the ocean, the breakfast, the solitude, the cliffs, and a span of deliberately aimless wandering. Then, on that veranda, I start to guess at the number of days in my life I have gazed on an ocean. And I realize I haven't; the sea has played no part in my life, my dreams, my longings——except when I was a child and dreamed of being a sailor. And beaches——I have always been mystified by those who lie on beaches, tried to guess what was happening behind the sunglasses. Now here I am with time to do nothing but stretch on a beach, wander for no reason, to saunter my way through a number of days, finding the pattern as I go along. To saunter, Thoreau tells me, is to go the roundabout way of the pilgrim, the one who is on his way to the *sainte terre*.

Below me in the creek the rocks, white, gray, black, are draped with long ropes of kelp that end in a bulb with a growth of thick hairs. The gulls are nearly tame here. A large gray one stands on the balcony a few inches away on one leg, long red beak curling to a black tip at the end. Below me a scrub jay, bright blue and gray, chirps loudly on a sage bush while his eye keeps vigil on every breath of wind. The sagebrush covers the bluff down to the rocks and sends its fragrance to mix with my eggs. Here and there bright yellow lizard's tail catches the light.

"It's not always so quiet," the waiter says. "Last year a police helicopter sighted some marijuana plants down on the bluff. You wouldn't believe the commotion. Chopper in the air, patrols decked out like riot police stomping down in the sage, and what do they find? Four marijuana plants. They stand clutching their haul proud as can be and have their photo taken. How much do you think that little operation must have cost them, for four plants? The grass industry is big here, two-point-five billion dollars big, the second-largest cash crop in California. What do they think they're doing using all those resources for four spindly bits of weed?"

"I guess Big Sur was always a place for experiment. It's the great American virtue," I said. "There must be dozens of stories stored in the rocks and the sage around here."

"You bet." The waiter laughed. "Henry Miller lit up Big Sur for a few years in the late forties, and one of his favorite companions was the chef here at Lucia. His name was Harvey, and he lived in a tent on the bluff with his wife and kids, played violin, tried to write and paint. Miller reckoned him the best talker ever, with an incredible knowledge of English literature, dreams of being a writer, and a creative flair as a chef. One night he found a penguin on the highway and cooked it for Miller. He came from the East Coast to Lucia to write, that being hardly realistic with a full-time job and a crowded tent. He always complained of writer's block. 'Forget that it's a sheet of white paper,' Miller encouraged him. 'Pretend it's an ear. Talk to it. Talk into it.' Harvey came back a fortnight later. It had worked. Another few weeks and he had thrown in his job at Lucia and gone back East. There's been so many like that who've passed through here, writers, artists, seekers after something or another, big dreamers, wild characters. Wait till you see Perce; he works the evening shift. You ever seen a tap-dancing waiter? He tap-dances his way round the tables and has the whole room gaping while he carries on a dialogue with himself and with clients, dancing all the while."

Seems like I'm one of those Big Sur dreamers now. Another hour with the view and I walk on down the road, follow my feet, come to a trail that draws me down steep cliffs into a dark green cleft in the hills. A jumble of rocks, sage, fennel, lizard's tail, spray, an endless ocean, and a sky lit now by a silver sun. I sit on that beach—Kirk Creek, it's called—and tremble to the rustle of the pebbles in the undertow, something being sucked out of me back to primordial waters. Waves tumble, flop over, crash down, fall softly, roar, rustle onto the shore. A harmless lapping and curling, and then an almighty wave with a crest of foam on its ridge shatters my lull and bursts me open, froth scattering traces all over my bare arms.

I walk on, and on again, and come upon a stretch of ancient marine terrace, Pacific Valley, with broad flat fields and cattle grazing and rock piles stuck out from the shore. The beaches are more accessible here, and I find a long white crescent, Sand Dollar Beach, to lounge on. Not a soul along the entire curve. The waves crash absolutely, unencumbered with doubt or hesitation. Their rumbling, roaring, curling, crashing lifts me also into dissolution; nothing to hold me now, not even faith, and just as I tip over the edge the seagull shrieks and kelp tendrils, huge organic forms ripped from the ocean floor, writhe in the falling wave. Then the water rolls even those thoughts away and I gaze at the rocks and the debris of kelp and sniff the salt on the wind. An enchanted coastline, yet everything so ordinary suddenly, rock and water. I saw then the rockiness of rock, wateriness of water there with the waves, the drying kelp, and a few little sand crabs.

That evening I went to the hot springs at Esalen Institute to watch the sun go down. Two rock pools of hot water perched above a kelp-strewn beach on the cliff, the ocean like stained glass now, purple and rose. People still flock here from all over the world to take courses on "mending the fragmented self," crosscultural shamanic practices, exploring the world of lucid dreaming, "managing your stress, your heart, and your life." The first human-potential center anywhere in the world, Esalen is now a model of respectability, its era of all-night encounter groups and hallucinogenic adventures confined to the history books. It is still a remarkable place, though, an experiential-learning institute that draws together an imaginative range of physical, psychological, and spiritual disciplines on a secluded cliff top among sequoias, along one of the wilder coastlines in the world. The Esselen were the Native Americans who lived in the area for some three thousand years, until they became extinct in the nineteenth century, and the hot springs on this cliff were known to be sacred to them.

Esalen is still a sacred place of sorts, a place of renewal, a latter-day Asclepius. In the hot baths under the dissolving sun I talked to an accountant from L.A. "I've been up here several times," he tells me, "but only ever to Esalen. Big Sur means Esalen to me. There's nothing for me outside of these gates." Well, there's something for me, though I am like him. I have stopped before only at Esalen, to get something done or undone, with a check-in and -out time. I have gazed on this coastline just from the baths, but that misty view insinuated itself into my mind and stayed there till one night in Sedona. This time I am encountering Big Sur and just passing by Esalen, for a bath and to meet an old friend for dinner. No, the deeper truth is, this coast has me feeling lonely already; I feel exposed, not only to the elements but to the sight of God, and I gravitate like a moth to the human warmth that I know is just down the road.

We dine at Deetjen's Big Sur Inn, where they bake a fine dish of yellowtail, locally caught, eaten beneath timbered ceilings, with plates on the wall, and a masseur behind the bar describing his craniosacral arts to the hotel guests with polished suavity. My friend lives in a wooden house with big ocean windows right on the cliff at Esalen. I wonder what impression it must make on a person to live and work in such natural splendor every day. "You know," she says, "at the end of nearly every day I turn and see a red line along the horizon and realize that I have missed the sunset again."

The next morning, up on the South Coast Rim dirt road, looking down over an ocean merged with sky and valleys tongued with thick white fog, I am glad again to be alive and alone; glad to be walking through the chaparral, the redwoods, the bay laurel and oak groves. Then round a bend in the track I see an old Chevy, doors open, six-pack on the passenger seat, music blaring, a red-nosed guy with hair to his shoulders lurching around with bottle in hand. Off on a side path two women are stumbling about holding on to each other for support. "Hi, I'm Carol," says one of them. "Isn't it beautiful up here on top of the world?" I muttered something in agreement as her

friend pulled her off in another direction, whispering forcefully in her ear. I left the Chevy riders behind and went on along toward Cone Peak, the high peak of the Santa Lucia Range, past ridges and valleys burned to a cinder in the recent forest fire, just a few charred stumps scattered across blackened hillsides. On through the fire zone, and for a few miles the only sound is the wind in the redwoods and the fluttering jays. Autumn leaves color here and there the conifer slopes that escaped the fire. Then a distant drone, a whir getting louder; a chopper drones by, following the path. The Marijuana

Elimination Unit glides over the treetops and circles back a few times before landing in a clearing over to my right. Two officers climb out, confer, wander about the clearing, and take off again. Perhaps I have been witness to the discovery of some magnificent haul that will hit the headlines the next day. Even these remote ridges are not safe from hidden eyes. I wonder who is watching me that I haven't seen; a coyote, an angel, a devil maybe.

Late in the day I drive up the path to the New Camaldoli Hermitage, just a few minutes from Lucia. The drive curls up a mountain and hovers over the Pacific, which is gray now with a slit of gold and some light pools on the far horizon. I had stayed more than once with the Camaldolese community in southern India. Following Camaldolese customs, the monks combine a life of solitude with the support of a community. Each monk has his own cottage, or cell, with its own garden and chapel, while they meet for worship in the community chapel four times a day. The monk in the bookshop is jolly, and I wonder if he is wearing a wig.

I pick up a book with a black cover called *The Tao of Big Sur*, a collection of poems by David Streeter. I know the name; I have seen it in the Esalen catalog. David Streeter is a body worker there. I read the Foreword, by Brother David Steindl-Rast. I had met Brother David at Esalen a year or so earlier, when he was there for a time in the capacity of spiritual adviser to the community. In his Foreword he says:

> *When I first met David Streeter, he was a candidate at the monastery in Big Sur. There was wild fire shining from his eyes. "If this one stays," I said, "monastic life will be ablaze in this community." When I visited again, he was still there, now wearing monk's robes. The orange trees entrusted to his care were a joy to behold. When I came again, fruit was rotting in the neglected orchard and David had left. . . . The poems in this volume were written by one for whom today's monastic conventions proved too narrow. These poems are romantic. Why not? They are obviously influenced by Ryokan and other Zen poets. There is fire in them, deep darkness too, nurturing darkness. They are a record of the other-than-candle variety of monks. . . .*

I flip through the pages, and a poem leaps out at me.

Today the wind
is pure ice
There is peace in it
somewhere and
my job is to find it
But right now I'm chilled to the bone.

The chapel is empty but for a few rows of chairs. Inside the door hangs a line of hooded robes, white and heavy. The altar, a square block of stone, stands in the heart of a shadowy rotunda. Above it hangs a small cross, suspended from the roof. I sit near the altar in low amber light that filters through windows of hammered glass. A peace here envelops the mind.

Soon a monk strides briskly in and begins to arrange the furniture for the next service. He runs his fingers along the back of a row of chairs, stopping here and there to align one an inch or two forward or backward. He takes the wooden lectern, moves it against the back wall, places a wrought iron candlestick where the lectern was, and lines both of them up with the altar. He steps smartly back a few inches, squints to confirm he has them exactly in line, adjusts the candlestick by half an inch, picks the lectern up, and sets it down squarely in exactly the same place, pats it, squints again, then proceeds to finger and pat the next line of chairs, and so on until every piece of furniture has been personally inspected and set right within a plan that clearly has no margin of error. His task over finally, the monk strides out like a victorious martial artist. I expected him to bow——to the chairs, that is——but that, I realize, would have been overstatement, an unnecessary flourish in this Zenlike procedure. Impressed with the zeal of this Christian monk, I wondered how men such as that could have let Streeter's orange trees fade. I wondered, too, what I had done, what I was doing, with the garden that had been entrusted to me.

The next evening, just before sunset, I found my way to Pfeiffer Beach, the one with the rock arches standing offshore and the light pouring through them like the gates to celestial fields. The gold turned to pink, purple, blood red, and moments later the light source had sunk in the ocean, the horizon stained now with a streak of violet. Not a soul there but me, a spangle of stars, the dark shape of cliffs, Jupiter trailing a star stream in tide pools. I gaze at the Big Dipper and remember it is we who have called it a name, given it a shape to carve it out from the rest of the firmament . I am here with all the world to myself, and I cry out suddenly, cry out with a life that has no name and that rises from my feet up through my body and involuntarily out of my throat. I am, of that there is no doubt. I am a mystery, a mystery I am. I am utterly alive in this darkness where the only sound is that of the untamable elements. Walking the shore in the dark, feeling my way slowly, I walk through the sand toward a tunnel of redwoods, the dark cut of rocks against stars. Fingering the soft bark I edge my way forward tree by tree and sit there, the life shivering through me, till the growing moon rises and shows me the way home.

When I step out of my door the next morning an African-American man is sharing a joke with a little girl outside the cabin next door. When she goes back inside he stoops to wipe his shoes, white ones with a metal tip on the heel. "How ya' doin' today?" he says and does a little two-step right there, as if to signal that today is a good day, no matter what. I'm doin' fine, and I tell him so, at which he tells me his name is Perce, the dancing waiter, and if I'd like to come by in the evening he'll be glad to serve me at table. That would be great, but I'm moving on today a little up the coast, don't quite know where.

A few miles past Esalen I see a sign for McEway Canyon, turn into the parking lot, and walk through the tunnel under the highway to look out over Saddle Rock Cove, where a thin waterfall pours from the cliff onto the beach below. The sea is turquoise in the horseshoe cove, and milky too with a long bed of kelp just beyond the offshore rocks. A smooth tight crescent of a beach, all sand, with barely a stone except by the cliffs, which seem to have been dropping their shingle on a regular basis. I love the way the water swells up over a lone rock, surrounds it, cascades over its edges, submerging it and letting it rise up again, a black gnarled thing in the sunlight. A battering it gets, like no one can know or even begin to understand what water does to rock, as it buries it and releases it again and again forever, till finally it grinds it down, sweeps it away, and all the while a red-tailed hawk pours by on the updraft.

Waves seem to dash themselves against this Saddle Rock with an ecstasy we can only begin to imagine. For when do we ever shower down in slivers of white light, never hitting the bottom, having emptied ourselves far into a clear sky long before then? Out to sea, the ocean swells heavy as oil paint on

a dark canvas even though the crests are tipped with silver. An elephant seal, like an overgrown slug, slithers off a rock below me into the waves.

Back along the trail into the canyon, the big reds quiet me down, root me to the brown earth with its twigs and leaves and rotting logs, and a stream that pours a hundred feet from a crevice in the rock, while sunpools light up the forest floor and round spiderwebs glisten in the light shafts that slip between the branches. An old barn of hand-split redwood crumbles into the earth, a memory of old McEway, who homesteaded here in the 1880s. Worn-out trunks hollowed and blackened by lightning stand beside more

youthful offspring that curve in a slow bend toward the light. Tiny birds snip at the mites along the dead branches, and the rocks here are mountain steady, even in the spray of the persistent stream, and trailing moss heavily. I never knew till I sat in McEway Canyon why people speak of redwoods differently. They store the peace of the ages and release it gently in a measure that humans can appreciate and feel grateful for.

I climb the trail to the ridge above the canyon, with more ridges cascading down to the shore beyond, a blue glaze on the ocean, a bluff of parched grass behind me, and a danger sign warning of unstable cliffs. A young garter snake slithers ahead of me in the gully in the trail, and two young men race past us, both heading for the higher peaks, one of them with stones in his backpack. I dawdle at the turns and lull to the drone of a light airplane and water in the canyon. The redwoods give way to tan oaks, then suddenly the trees stop; the ridge carves a line against the clear sky and the canyon already far below. I sit on the ridge looking over the water, and I realize after an hour or two that I have been feeding there, unconsciously collecting radiance through my eyes.

When the ocean turns pink finally, I scramble back down the darkening path and head on up the highway past Loma Vista gas station and café. Hilary, an Englishman, has recently bought Loma Vista from the Post family, one of the first clans to homestead in Big Sur and owners of the Loma

Vista property for 150 years. On down the road is Ripplewood Resort, a jumble of wood cabins, and I take one.

The Ripplewood café is closed for the evening so I go to the Ferndale Inn just round a curve in the road and discover the local haunt, the inn full of men with bushy beards and large bellies, along with a dozen Mexicans, local store employees drinking beer from cans. The bar lady gives me a glass of wine for free because it is the end of the bottle, and two minutes later roars through the room pushing one of the bushy men before her screaming that she's had enough, he's got to be out of here, and never to come back. The whole room explodes with laughter and everybody whistles and claps.

A woman starts a conversation with me, telling me how she lived with a man in a parachute in the Northern Territory of Australia before she settled down in Big Sur. Here, her "thing" is rubbish.

"I go out on Pfeiffer Beach and pick it all up. That beach has been such a sanctuary for me I can't bear to see it desecrated. The store owner gives me trash bags and I spend the day there. You wouldn't believe how much I pick up. And you know, the funny thing is, I normally have sciatica in my back, but when I'm on that beach bending down all the time, I never get so much as a twinge. My friend says you can never feel pain when you are sharing your love. I don't know, but I don't get sciatica on Pfeiffer."

The next morning at breakfast in the Ripplewood café everyone is reading the papers and talking about the election, it being November of 1996. I sit on a bar stool with vines painted up the stem. The food comes out piled high and I remember again that this is America and it is normal to feel daunted by the size of the servings.

"Hey Bob, how are you doin' today?" The waitress is greeting one of the regulars, a three-hundred-pounder who drives the school bus.

"You know what? I'm feeling like shit." The room goes quiet. The waitress is caught off guard. Her head drops a little, and in a voice that begins to sound real, she says, "Really? Well, I've got to say I don't feel so good myself this morning."

"Yeah, I just had twenty minutes of bad-mouthing down the phone from the administrative office. They say I didn't hand in my docket last week saying how many kids I had on my bus. This job is getting more paperwork by the year, and I'm about ready to stuff it."

"What about your kids, Bob, and the pension?"

"Yeah, well, fuck it, it's off my chest, now you guys have listened to me. You know who I voted for? I voted for no one. I ain't gonna vote for the two parties while they don't let Perot come in on the debates. Heck, this is meant to be a free country—that's what we're all so proud of, isn't it?—and Perot's not allowed to talk."

They are all still arguing the point when I leave to visit the library next door. The Big Sur library, a kind of classroom with a couple of computer terminals, was empty, and I got to talking with the librarian. She told me she was a poet and a painter, and that this was a fill-in job. She had just left her husband of twenty-seven years because she had come to realize that truth is the highest good and she had to face all the denial that had kept their marriage together for so long. Leaving, she said, was wonderful and terrible. She often wakes up now next to her new partner dreaming of her old one. She reads me one of her poems. It's good, full of images of these hills and streams. She shows me a painting. Big Sur collects artists like other places gather moss.

The other library in Big Sur is Henry Miller's, back near Deetjen's Big Sur Inn. On the door is a note from Miller:

HOW TO BE AN ARTIST

STAY LOOSE. LEARN TO WATCH SNAILS. PLANT IMPOSSIBLE GARDENS. MAKE LITTLE SIGNS THAT SAY "YES" AND POST THEM ALL OVER YOUR HOUSE. MAKE FRIENDS WITH UNCERTAINTY.

I met an artist there too, George Choley. He does landscapes, rich colors in a naive style, popular with the local galleries. George drove out here from Michigan in the early fifties in a twenty-year-old Model A Ford, got a girl pregnant and stayed, worked for Miller up on Partington Ridge, and still lives there himself today, a gleam in his eyes now as there ever was. "An incredible presence," said George of Henry. "The bar would be quiet, Henry would come in, and suddenly everyone would be laughing and talking like there was no tomorrow. He'd stir up conversations out of nothing that would go on for hours. It was the same at his house at mealtimes. People were always dropping in and not leaving."

Heading north finally, I spend my last day in Big Sur on the beach at

Molera, but just before then I gaze at the wall of collage over the counter at the Big Sur Stores:

PAGAN WAYS LIVE ON

SAINTHOOD NOT REQUIRED

WHEREVER YOU GO THERE YOU ARE

DO NOT LIKE DO NOT DISLIKE ALL WILL THEN BE CLEAR

I CAN'T REMEMBER THE LAST TIME I FELT THIS WAY

WHERE IS BIG SUR?

YOU ARE CORDIALLY INVITED TO FEEL SMALL AND INSIGNIFICANT

NEXT REST STOP 40 MILES

Behind the cash register a candle burns on a little altar with images of Christ, Buddha, and the Dalai Lama. The store owner, a lean man in denim with graying hair down to his shoulders and a face that has seen a fair share of life, is commiserating with Elma, an ample woman in her forties whose house has burnt down in the recent forest fire, there being no fire insurance in Big Sur.

The pain and the beauty. Immersed in beauty, I am there by the shore. Big Sur River sneaks out over Molera beach through a delta of mossed shingle. The big rock of Point Sur lies over a few green fields, the first to reach the ocean since Pacific Valley, some thirty miles south. Slender bars of cloud along the horizon. Behind, the bluffs fold over one another like so many tender lovers. Never have I seen dolphins wheeling in the light like this, playing in pairs, tumbling in the waves, diving among the gulls, so much larger, more potent than I. Driftwood in heaps, bleached tree trunks, planks of old redwood, stray branches like whitened bone, turned into shelters in the lee of the cliffs. The stones here glisten with quartz, and I put two in my bag, a white one and a black, two eggs to hatch in another world. What is happiness? This that I am now, nothing to hold on to, no great elation, no inspired plan or project, just this that I am now, a belonging to present time, and gratitude from right down below.

The Way of the Animal Powers

*Shamans tell us that, were meaning to come to us fully
unveiled, it would turn us into it, that is, it would kill us.
This is why we must content ourselves with whispers
and glimmers of meaning.*

— MALIDOMA SOMÉ

Through Tony Pascoe's study window lies a perfect English view: Kelston Round Top, a knoll crowned with a clump of trees, rises gently from the far bank of the river Avon, which flows by the gates of Pascoe's family home, near Bath. The mythic green and pleasant land survives here still, at the dawn of the third millennium. Inside, the study walls are thick with hunting trophies, not the local deer but buffalo, lion, wildebeest, impala. Propped in a corner by the window, the long blade of a Masai spear catches the afternoon light. Tony Pascoe lives in two worlds. His family lives by the Avon, while he spends every other month in Tanzania, running safaris in the Serengeti.

I had been vaguely aware for years that there was a missing dimension in my relationship with the natural world. I had never encountered an animal more wild than a fox or a badger. European heraldry reminds us that the old continent was once as rich with wolf and bear as America was in the eighteenth century.

Today, we live sequestered from the primal forces of nature. It was not that I was tempted to flirt with danger; I simply felt the absence from my experience of our nearest neighbors in the circle of life. For countless millennia, humans and animals have lived alongside each other in mutual respect. Respect was bound up with awe and dread, and these are not emotions to be evoked by a sheep or a donkey. Domestic animals, like ourselves, have their original wildness hidden beneath warm coats.

Pascoe's study proved to be my antechamber to Africa. As a child of four he knew already that he wanted to be a game warden when he grew up. By the age of ten he had a pet kestrel, and in his teens he became a falconer. He went to Africa in his twenties and worked for some years as a warden, but eventually had to leave his work in Kenya because of the Africanization policy of the time. Now he runs a company that takes people on balloon flights over the Serengeti, the largest game reserve in Africa.

I could just imagine it, champagne at a hundred feet in the company of rich tourists from around the world—the very antithesis of what I had in mind. Yet a mutual friend had urged me to meet Pascoe. "A very unusual man. Don't be fooled by the balloons. If anyone can help you organize your own wildlife journey, it will be him," she assured me. "He's leaving tomorrow, so you'd better be quick."

Later that same afternoon I was sitting in his study.

"I don't want to go in a Jeep, either alone or with others," I explained. I don't just want to *see* wildlife; I want to lock eyes, feel an exchange, a relationship with them and with the surrounding environment. I want to camp and walk through the bush alone with a guide."

"That is exactly what I would love to do myself." Pascoe smiled. "I know just the man to take you. But while you are there I think you should also have some contact with the Masai, the people of the land. They are as much a part of the spirit of the place as the wildlife. If you like, I could arrange a walking journey through Masai country, and then a walking safari with my friend."

I quickly agreed. Africa, I was going to learn, has something unique to offer the modern world; it speaks to a forgotten level of the imagination, and the people are as much a part of that ancient dimension as the natural world they inhabit. The following week I completed a team training program I was running for Ford of Britain, and took a plane to Nairobi. At 5 P.M. on Friday

I was in the corporate world, and at 10 A.M. on Saturday I was hurtling toward the Tanzanian border through purple mountains and miles of savanna in a shuttle bus whose driver was determined to break the land speed record. The road was empty, save for the occasional herd boy and his cattle. At the border, Masai men and women thrust their beadwork through the open windows of the buses, while Kenyan exchange bureaus relieved me of more dollars than I had sense. Four hours later, my eyes full of rolling land and vast sky, gray still at the end of the rainy season, I clambered off the bus at Arusha, Tanzania's second-largest town.

Arusha sprawls in the lee of Mount Meru, Tanzania's second-highest mountain after Kilimanjaro. It has all the spirit of a frontier town, now that Nyerere's socialist dream is a failure of the past and capitalist ethics are in the ascendancy. In the early nineties, the shops would have nothing on display except perhaps the occasional pair of shoes or pack of sugar. A huge black-market economy thrived in the back room, away from the eyes of state employees. Now foreign currency is easily available on any street corner; street traders hawk music cassettes, international newspapers, tourist trinkets, and solicit customers for safari companies. The shops, many of them owned by the growing Asian community, are full of electrical goods. The traffic, still refreshingly sparse, is almost entirely four-wheel drive, much of it the property of the safari business, which the Asians and the expatriate white community share between them.

But this development is still new and tentative. While the other East African countries developed their tourist economies decades ago, socialist Tanzania remained grandly aloof from such profit-driven initiatives. One of the results of this high-minded policy is that the country is still the second or third poorest in the world. Until recently, the authorities simply made it too complicated to set up business there. Even now they have no intention of becoming another Kenya. Foreign enterprises need to invest a minimum of $500,000 to set up business, so safari companies are unlikely to move in in a hurry. Speculative development is viewed with deep caution, and an incredible eleven percent of the country is designated as national park, which protects both the wildlife there and the land itself. For the time being, Tanzania remains the undeveloped frontier of African big game, and this, Tony Pascoe had assured me, was one of the reasons he would recommend it to me.

Tony was waiting for me at the hotel, a concrete block owned by the government and managed by the French Novotel group. "Everything is arranged," he told me, over a Tusker beer (Kenyan import). "You start out the day after tomorrow with a team of Masai. I know you only wanted to walk with one guide, and you will be doing that later with Paul Oliver, but I'm afraid my contact with the Masai insisted that you take a team. You have to take your own food and water, and that needs donkeys. The donkeys need their masters, and you also need a cook because the guide would not see that to be part of his duties."

I was too tired to think of the implications of Tony's admission, and my attention was diverted when he suggested we spend the following day together driving into Arusha National Park, an area not far from the town and one quite different from the land I would be walking through later. Those few hours with the man I had met by the Avon showed me how intimately he was at home in the wild. The national park is on the rim of an old volcano, one of many, like Meru and Kilimanjaro, that surge out of the floor of the Great Rift Valley. Its slopes are covered in dense jungle, and the foliage and altitude combine to make its own unique weather conditions—cold swirling mists when we were there. Colobus monkeys with fluffy white tails swung from tree to tree, giraffe trotted elegantly across the track, waterbuck merged into the foliage. Wild fig trees twisted round other species, sucking the life from them, expanding out of the husks of what used to be canopy trees.

The track climbed to the crater rim, and there below us was a flat green plain dotted with buffalo. A family of baboons emerged on the tree by our Land Rover. Tony pressed his face to the window and raised his eyebrows several times in quick succession while pursing his lips at the same time. The nearest baboon pounded its fists on the branch and retreated a few steps. Then Tony made a simpering sound and the baboon ran a few steps closer to us. "Baboon language," he explained. "What I did first was to imitate their threat gestures, and then I followed that with their friendship sound."

As we drove back down from the rim, Tony suddenly stopped the car and motioned to me to get out. He pointed to a file of large red ants crossing the track. "Soldier ants. They eat everything in their path. See their pincers? When they bite they don't let go. The Masai hold them to an open wound so that their pincers act like stitches." He picked one up and it immediately dug into his finger. He squeezed its body and pulled it away, showing me the two red incisions it had left behind in his skin.

A small black-and-white bird with a long tail landed on a bush in front of us.

"That harmless little shrike is known as the butcher bird. It catches mice and lizards and hangs them out to dry on a thornbush. The bush serves as its larder. Be careful of that plant behind you with the leaves like rhubarb. It will sting you even through thick trousers."

His warning was too late. I retained the memory of that African rhubarb for several hours afterward. I was beginning to realize that I had stepped into a land where every life form seemed to personify vibrant intensity. Wildlife, it was beginning to dawn on me, didn't just mean lion or elephant. The local bees and scorpions, I was told, delivered a sting that was painful for at least twenty-four hours. It was all rather different from Ford.

The next morning a driver arrived to take me to the departure point for the walk through Masai country. Half an hour out of Arusha we turned onto a track and wound up through some mud-hut villages onto an escarpment. The track petered out and we came to a halt under an acacia tree. Below us a sea of grass rolled away to a far horizon. My lungs filled with a new air, my heart and eyes lifted to accommodate the great space. Just along the ridge four men were trying to load four donkeys with jerry cans of water and tenting equipment. One donkey was dragging a man along on the end of its tether, another was running off toward us with someone in chase, and the other two men were doubled up in laughter.

This, I was told, was my team. They were Wa'Arusha, Masai-speaking people who had settled on the fringes of the town, most of whom had been educated in Christian schools. One of those who had been laughing straightened and came toward me, hand outstretched. He had the long, handsome features of the Nilotic Masai, who had migrated down here from Ethiopia and Somalia in the sixteenth century. His name was Emmanuel, he said with a self-conscious grin, and he was my guide. My spirits were going up and down like a barometer. Before me spread some of the most uplifting country I had seen in a long while. Before me, too, stood my companions for the next week or so. They were clearly going to have fun.

I remembered my time with Sliman, my guide in the Sinai, and how I had had to resort to various ploys to keep a distance between his chatter with his cousin, his radio, and me. This crew were double the number, which almost certainly meant quadruple the chatter. This was why I had wanted to walk with just one guide; I had also wanted a companion who still lived the life of a Masai pastoralist, rather than someone who was the hired hand of a Western tourist company and who probably lived uneasily between both worlds. I was almost certainly asking too much, the victim perhaps of my own romantic fantasy; a true pastoralist would never have taken a white man walking through his land in any case. There and then I determined to manage with what had been offered me.

Two hours later they had finally loaded the donkeys, and we set off down the ridge onto the open plain. Mount Meru drifted in and out of view behind the clouds to the north, its flat top startlingly clear every now and then against the pearl of the sky. We weaved in and out of acacia groves, twice startling a family of giraffe. In the early afternoon we came across a *boma*, a group of round mud huts encircled by a thorn stockade. A few women stood at the entrance watching us pass. Emmanuel exchanged some words with them, while they and I looked each other up and down with the

inquisitiveness of two different species who, on appearances, had no real reference for each other's existence. Bead earrings hung heavily from their elongated earlobes, copper and silver bracelets adorned much of their lower arms and legs. This was their land, I was the alien, and I had caught myself gawping at them like so many curious specimens. What business did I have being here? I wondered—the usual question after a few days of walking, but rare so early on.

A few minutes later, as we went on through the acacias, two young Masai warriors came loping toward us from among the trees with a gait that seems unique to them—a lilting, dipping movement, like a ship in a light head wind—spears in their left hands, right hands outstretched in greeting, broad grins on their faces. So alive, so vital, they evaporated any lingering thoughts of gloom I may have been harboring. Their uncut hair, braided and tied back, was dyed with ocher. Their torsos gleamed in the afternoon light; a short broadsword hung at each waist; they were clothed, as are all Masai men, in a simple red cloth, one of them in a tartan variety, and some intricate beadwork about the neck. Nothing could be said, but no words were needed. As our hands met, race, culture fell away in the momentary exchange of life with life. I remembered what Tony Pascoe had said, how the Masai are a part of this land just as the animals are. In that moment, I too felt a part of the land, of the earth, and in that articulate simplicity we recognized each other.

From midadolescence until well into his twenties, the Masai warrior, known as the *murran,* enjoys a unique sense of brotherhood with his peers and a degree of respect from the rest of the community that would be the envy of any teenager. Masai culture is rigidly divided into age status. A male is first a herd boy, with the task of tending the family cattle, then a bachelor *murran,* during which time he and his peers are a society within a society, free to go their own way as long as they maintain unfailing respect for their elders; then as a married elder he gives up the freedom and adornments of youth, his mother cutting his hair in an often emotional ceremony; finally, as a senior elder, he will take more responsibility within the clan and help to make decisions on behalf of the community. Women follow the natural progression from unmarried girl to wife to widow without the ceremony enjoyed by the men.

What a luxury, now almost extinct in the developed world: to know your place indisputably through the passage of life and to be sustained in the conviction of your identity by an unfailing solidarity with your peers. Individuality, especially for a *murran,* means little among the Masai. It is the age group he is in that gives a Masai his substance, and it shines through his vitality and proud bearing.

On we trekked through the long grass for hours, beyond the last acacias in the direction of a ridge that curved away in front of us. My socks were festooned with grass seed and hairs, and every step pressed a thousand tiny pins into my ankles. Finally I took my socks off and found the grass much kinder to my bare ankles. Emmanuel led me up the ridge while the donkeys went a longer, gentler way. The top was another flat plain, sloping gradually to the north.

We could see at least forty miles in every direction. Volcanic hills were scattered everywhere between great stretches of grassland. The sun, low on the horizon now, sent a sliver of light through pink-and-silver cloud banks. A dozen impala, deerlike creatures with spiraling horns and two brown stripes on their rear, skipped through the grasses in front of us. Two secretary birds, frumpy specimens in gray plumage, strutted off importantly toward a lone tree.

Emmanuel was a few hundred yards ahead of me. I was hanging back, savoring a taste of aloneness on this first day in the bush. It was then that I saw it, a wildebeest some three hundred yards off, facing me with its nose to the wind. I cannot adequately convey what the sight of that animal did for me. Unaware as I was at the time of its timorous nature, it was to my eyes like some huge black bull, its horns splayed out against the sky, front legs in that pugnacious stance known so well to matadors in the Spanish ring. It was magnificent, utterly in its element, and it sent a shiver of life through every cell of my body. I stood and gazed at it in wonderment, full of gratitude for whatever turn of fate had brought me here to this extraordinary land. Finally, it turned and cantered away, though for a moment my eyes continued to see its apparition in the place where it had stood.

We camped that evening on the escarpment. Goat sizzled on the fire, and the night air was filled with my team's banter. Nothing mattered; the sky was lit with more stars than I had seen even in the Sahara. To the south hung a great sign that held my eye: I was under the light of the Southern Cross for the first time in my life. We put a light outside each tent to ward off animals, and I lay down finally, the thought winds settled in me. A spontaneous prayer breathed from my lips as I was on the edge of sleep:

Spirit of this land,
protect us.
Spirits of the Masai people,
protect us.
Spirit of the animal powers,
protect us.

That night the donkeys screamed twice, probably to warn off the hyena. The next day we followed the slope of the escarpment toward the east under a sky the color of tin. We walked the whole afternoon through acacia woods, and I noticed how my preference was for the big view of the open plain. In the woods we were pushing through thick undergrowth, and I had to keep closer to the team so as not to lose my way. We saw no animals, though we passed termite mounds, tall sand castles with chimneys, usually in the shelter of a tree. I was reminded of something I had read, that there is more flesh under the ground in Africa than there is above it. An incredible and somehow unsavory thought, that those white larvae added up to more meat than all the hundreds of thousands of zebra, wildebeest, cats, elephants, and humans put together.

We camped within the sound of cattle bells, in front of a yellow-fever tree with two hornbills courting each other in its branches. The tree got its name from nineteenth-century Europeans who imagined that because the tree was the yellowy green color that characterized the illness, the fever came from the tree. Wrong. It came from the water that was usually near the tree.

We spent two nights by the yellow-fever tree. In the morning I strolled some twenty minutes away from camp toward an outcrop of red rock that jutted above the acacias. Birdsong of a hundred varieties filled the air. "Superb starlings"—that is their name—flashed from tree to tree, all brilliant blue with golden breasts. A type of guinea fowl startled me every few hundred yards by waiting to the last second before squawking away from under my feet. Over them all a mystery bird sounded a long, clear note.

As I walked on I became increasingly aware of my aloneness. I noted the nearest tree to leap into in the event of the sudden appearance of a buffalo. If I saw a big cat, I reminded myself, all I had to do was to stand still. That was the theory. Those rocks ahead of me seemed to exert a strange magnetic presence. The land spoke strongly here. I could see a skeleton in a large termite mound—the two eye sockets stared blindly in my direction, a large nose cavity just below them. The intensity of the birdsong only added to the potency of the place.

I walked as far as the first rock, then something, perhaps simple fear, drew me back. Those rocks were the unknown, and a sunny rock was a favorite haunt of lion. This was still all very new; I turned back toward camp. After twenty minutes I began to realize that one acacia looks much like another. I knew the rocks were slightly to the right of camp, but after half an hour I realized that I was completely lost. I call out. No answer. Louder. I curse my arrogance for taking this land so lightly. This is not some television documentary; this land where I presume to wander at my leisure with nothing but a water bottle is alive with eyes that I cannot see.

Respect, my son had said just before I left, is what Africans have to teach us. *Nkanyit,* the Masai call it—respect for their customs, for the elders, and for the land. *Nkanyit* is the basis of their culture. And here am I wandering up and down, not knowing what else to do but to keep a sight on the rocks to the north. They seem farther away now than they were from the camp, but I don't know; difficult to tell. Isn't this, though, the essence of a sacred journey? The thought occurred to me suddenly and opened my self-concern onto a larger perspective. The aimless wandering the Sufis call a pilgrimage. Is this meandering around in acacia woods so very different from a typical day in my life? I have rarely had any clear idea of where I am going, and am coming to learn that in the deepest sense, it doesn't really matter. My life has been a long apprenticeship to trust.

Just then I caught sight of a patch of white among the trees off more in the direction of the rocks: my towel, hung out to dry on the tent. I sauntered toward the camp; the crew were fiddling with the fire; my mind readjusted to its familiar conventions. Whatever the larger picture, I lay down under the yellow-fever tree with unequivocal relief.

That afternoon Emmanuel led me to a *boma* that was a mile or so through the trees. Several *murran* were walking away from the thicket enclosure until one of them turned and saw us approaching. They stopped and waited, shards of red against the acacia green. We admired each other's artifacts, they my camera, I the beadwork their wives had adorned them with. One had a small bottle attached to his necklace, the others had small leather pouches strung from theirs.

One of them said something to Emmanuel. "They want to know how much you will pay to photograph them," he translated. Before I could address the question, one of them had drawn *1000* in the sand. Another added an extra zero. Then one of them changed the *1* to a *2*. I hate my camera in moments like this. But business is business anywhere in the world, and the Masai were notorious for selling their image at every opportunity. And why not? My very presence there invited such a response. "Either become an anthropologist or an aid worker, give five years of your life to these people, or stay away," I muttered in self-reproach.

The photograph question unresolved, above all in my own mind, we passed through the opening into the *boma*. There were several mud huts, each with its own mini-enclosure. Emmanuel told me that each hut was the family home of a son of the father, and that the overall enclosure constituted one extended family. One of the sons ushered me into his hut. Through the

gloom I could make out three sleeping platforms—one for the men, one for the women, and one for the small children. The kitchen was a few pots round a fire pit. Traditionally, the Masai eat only the milk and blood of their cattle, usually mixed. Sometimes a goat is killed, and more commonly now, they have taken to cultivating maize.

When we emerged from the hut an old man was outside, leaning on his spear. The *murran* had become less boisterous, and one of them muttered something to Emmanuel about not mentioning their demand for money. This was their father, the chief of that clan. He too had a bottle dangling from his neck, and he touched it as he said something to Emmanuel. "He's asking if you have any tobacco. They like to use snuff, which is what the bottle is for."

On learning that I had no tobacco, he asked if I had any medicine for his stiff knee. Not having that either, not having anything in my pockets to offer in exchange for their hospitality, or any conversation beyond the facile admiration of their attire, I felt the most honorable course was to withdraw to our camp and to content myself with the walking. We shook hands warmly, the *murran* the image of respectability now. Though they are given a long rope, the *murran* are always under the ultimate threat of the elder's curse, which can mean ostracism and even death.

Later that evening I heard a Masai woman singing. Her voice cut the air and also something in me that needed to give. The Masai sing, I had been told, to ensure the protection of God's presence. That night, under the yellow-fever tree, I had a dream that shook me awake. I was among the community I had been part of until my first wife and I had separated. I was making a sort of confession to them: how I wanted to forgive and to receive forgiveness in order to heal the rift between myself, my ex-wife, and our son and the community. I was saying how one of the most sacred journeys was the mending of the family hoop, and how the medicine was forgiveness.

When I finished talking I had the physical sensation of long-forgotten parts of me, like shadows or ghosts, returning both to myself and to the whole community. But the community wasn't just the people in present time; it was all those people who had gone before us, the family lines of my ex-wife and myself, and also of others we were close to in the present.

When I awoke it was with the intimation that all my extended family, past, present, and perhaps even the future, were there with me then, in the

African savanna, that they always had been with me, and I with them, and I had never really known it. And I knew somehow that it was no accident that it was in Africa that I had had such a dream.

Africa, of all places on earth, is the land of the ancestors, not because of ancestral worship, which is common to all ancient cultures—Africa is the land where the human race began. Less than a hundred miles from where I was crawling out of my tent was the Olduvai Gorge, a twenty-five-mile gash in the Serengeti Plain that has yielded the most spectacular and continuous evidence of humanity's origins and cultural development. Professors Louis

and Mary Leakey began a lifelong career there in 1931, uncovering evidence of a 2-million-year history of the human family. In 1960 their son Jonathan found the remains of *Homo habilis,* man the toolmaker and the first true human, 1.75 million years old. They discovered *Homo erectus,* 1.5 million years old, in the same year. The African Middle Stone Age, two hundred thousand years ago, is now associated with the emergence of our subspecies, *Homo sapiens sapiens.* The Leakeys also discovered the oldest human structure known, the remains of a stone shelter built a million years ago in Olduvai Gorge. Africa—I felt it in my marrow that morning—invites us to enter the primordial circle of life, which has never been broken.

After an hour of walking on through the acacias, I had forgotten the Leakeys and was thoroughly absorbed in some anxiety over my mortgage. Every so often I would shake myself free from the grip of the mind and bring my awareness to the rise and fall of my belly; walking and breathing, walking and breathing. Then back to the mortgage, or to thinking that I'd had enough of tramping through the scrub with four village boys whose harmless banter disturbed my self-absorption.

Only later that day did I see the obvious: that circle of life I had seen—everyone is in it. These boys I am traveling with, they are in it; they have never been out of it. Their banter is in it too; it's a part of What Is, and as long as I sullenly struggle against things as they are, I am keeping myself outside of life. And that's painful. I can't control the world and its noises. My energy would be better spent in changing what I can, and one place to start could be my own reactions.

We came across a well in the afternoon that was the only water source for miles around. Masai women had walked miles with their donkeys to fetch water for their families. One of them complained to Emmanuel that we were taking their water without permission and that the water there had to last them until the next rainy season. They argued back and forth for twenty minutes, more for the sake of the audience of Masai men than the justice of their position. It all ended with laughter and a few friendly gibes, the audience slapping their thighs and drawing long breaths over their snuff bottles.

Another two days of walking and we were in sight of our final camp, which was under a ridge with a view of hundreds of miles of great space in all directions. While the crew set up the tents, I scrambled up the rocks. Across the plain to the north was Longido Mountain and the Kenyan border. In the other direction I could just make out the shape of Ol-Doinyo Lengai——the "mountain of God," the Masai call it——the only active volcano left in Tanzania.

The sun is breaking through the clouds to shimmer the land; zebra, a hundred of them, are moving slowly through the trees toward Longido. I become aware of a silence beneath the wind and the birdsong. It takes hold of my mind. I close my eyes. When I open them again, an impala is gazing down at me from a rock above. I move from my own rock to a warmer one a little below. Silence works on the body cell by cell. Three crested birds with foot-long tails swoop by me. A frog peers over a rock and ducks when I look his way. White butterflies flit from flower to flower.

I close my eyes again and sit there for much of the afternoon. I think of my father, who would often sit for hours, eyes closed, in his chair, and I a feisty teenager, lamenting his idleness. Finally, I get up to go, and raise my hands in thanks. The first part of my journey is almost over. I came here to encounter the animal powers, but first Africa gave me something else: it threw me a line from the ancestral web and reeled me deeper into the human community.

The next morning we walked across the plain toward Longido until we met the road to Arusha. Two Land Rovers were waiting for us, one to take the crew back to town and the other to take me on through Tarangire

National Park to Paul Oliver's camp, which serves as a base for his walking safaris. Three hours later we stopped in a small village of tents, and Paul Oliver came out to greet me.

He was a tall, athletic Englishman in his early forties, with the informality that often accompanies those used to living in more than one culture. Drinks in hand, he led me to the shade of a sausage tree. The seed pods that give it its name hung heavily from every branch. Between one and two feet long, and four or five inches in girth, they can be dangerous missiles in the wrong season. We were in a clearing below some rocks, a mile or two from the national park, and on the migration route that the animals followed to and from the Tarangire River. Several large green tents merged easily with the foliage. One was a dining room, one an office, another a library. The rest were guest quarters.

Paul had been in Africa for fifteen years. Like Tony Pascoe, he had dreamed of living there since childhood, and in his twenties he had driven overland in the converted truck that was his home for several years. He covered the length and breadth of the continent during that time, always with an eye out for a country to settle in. He finally decided on Tanzania because it was still the most undeveloped of the East African states, and that area of the continent, with its rolling savanna and wildlife, was the terrain that most touched his imagination. His choice of occupation was simple: he would do what he loved best and put his knowledge of the wild to good use by taking people on walking safaris, a new alternative to the conventional "fly by in a Land Rover with your camera" variety.

Before we left the shade of the sausage tree I found myself asking the inevitable question. "Have you ever had any close encounters?"

"I spent a couple of hours up a tree a few years ago with two guests. We had surprised some buffalo, and the tree was our only way out. I always carry a radio, so help is never too far away. I was chased for more than a kilometer recently by a herd of elephants, but I was in the Jeep at the time, so I was able to outpace them. I have only ever had to kill an animal once in five years. That was a lioness. We surprised her in the grass. If you stand your ground, a cat will usually slip away. But she didn't. For half an hour neither of us moved. Then suddenly she came for me. I had no choice but to shoot. I can tell you I cried on and off for a week after that. I even considered giving the whole thing up. But some old-timers brought me round. They said, 'Look,

Paul, if you're going to do walking safaris, you have to expect a situation like that every few years. It's part of the job. That's what life is like out here.'

"So I always tell people I walk with that there is bound to be an element of risk. Yet in reality, no species, with the occasional exception of humans, is looking for confrontation. The rule here is one of avoidance. You can be sure that when we walk out tomorrow, there will far more eyes on us than we are aware of. All animals have known for thousands of years that their greatest danger comes in the shape of a human being. If we follow a few basic guidelines, we shouldn't run into any trouble. If we meet a cat, we stand and face it. If we come across elephant, we try and outmaneuver them, give them a wide berth. If we meet buffalo, we run. That increases the critical distance at which they feel safe, and minimizes any sense of threat. Buffalo are responsible for more fatalities than any other large animal, yet they are bovines, essentially nervous. If we don't give them cause for concern by getting too close, they generally keep to their grazing. At the same time, I have to say that every situation is unique, depending on the individual animal. We can never know what will happen, but I am sure you will enjoy it."

I am sure I will enjoy it. It is six-thirty the next morning, and Paul is leading me along a sand gully with steep tree banks. Elephant tracks and leopard droppings are everywhere. After an hour we climb the bank and pick our way through waist-high grass. Suddenly, just where I am about to place my right foot, a black snake, six feet long and several inches thick, rears up in my path.

"Run!" shouts Paul, who is a few yards ahead of me. I run, or scramble, away to the left. The snake disappears.

"Well done," Paul breathes with a gasp and a laugh. "That was a black spitting cobra. If you had stayed there it would have spat in your eyes and blinded you in a few minutes. They are deadly accurate. They always go for the eyes. I'm not sure whether to say you are fortunate or unlucky to have seen one. It's quite rare, because snakes usually disappear before we even know they have been there. He must have been asleep."

From then on I, for my part, was as awake as I had ever been. This was no gentle stroll through some country lane. There is nothing easier while walking than to slip into daydream, but here I needed all my senses, and I needed them now. Paul was constantly scanning the horizon and the trees, looking for the black hulk of buffalo or elephant and the dark, stumplike image of a lion in the grass.

Within the hour he stopped and pointed to a ridge in the distance. I could see nothing. He handed me his binoculars. "Look for a black line." Finally I caught sight of them—half a dozen buffalo standing end to end, their spines just visible through the long grass. One turned and sniffed the wind in our direction. Paul pointed us along another way.

We reached an outcrop of rocks and gazed over the grass plain to isolated mountains on the horizon; a band of green swamp curved away off to our left. Paul pointed out the dust cloud that was moving across it in the wake of a herd of elephants. Three zebra were running through the grass below us; a family of giraffe were nibbling at the upper foliage of an acacia. "You hear that birdcall? It's a honeyguide, and it's calling to us."

Paul scrambled down from the rocks toward the birdcall. A small bird flew out of a nearby acacia and flitted off to one further into the plain. When we caught up with it, if flew on to another tree, and finally brought us to a magnificent baobab, a tree unique to Africa that looks as if it must move at night. (It is said that Tolkien had the idea of the hobbit from seeing a baobab.) Pegs had been driven into its trunk to form a ladder to the top.

"The honeyguide leads men, honey badgers, and baboons to wild honey," Paul explained. "It would be stung to death if it went near the bees' nest on its own, so it shows other species who eat honey to the nest, and when they have broken it open, the honeyguide comes along afterward and eats up what is left. The bees almost always choose a baobab, and the Masai have been collecting honey for centuries. Some of the peg ladders you see on baobabs are generations old. They smoke the bees out by burning elephant dung, and over time they have developed a near immunity to bee stings."

The baobab was purplish, with a gnarled and knobby trunk, conical in shape, with branches that sprouted out at odd angles as if it had been given an electric shock. Elephants had stripped some bark to find moisture, and had rubbed parts of the trunk smooth. This baobab was hollow, though far from dead.

"Most of them are hollow," commented Paul. "Then, many of them are extremely old; I mean thousands of years, in some cases. They are a favorite hiding place for ivory smugglers." He showed me the mango-shaped fruit; the white seeds, he said, had ten times more vitamin C than an orange. We sucked some like lozenges, and carried on down an old hunter's track in the direction of the swamp.

Superb starlings swooped over our heads, and franklins, partridgelike creatures, ran gawkily in our path. We were near the edge of the swamp now, and strutting through the reeds came a gray, long-necked bird, not dissimilar to a turkey but larger. "A kori bustard," Paul said. "The heaviest flying bird in the world. Up ahead is a water hole where we will have some lunch."

The water hole, perhaps a hundred yards long, was streaked with the slivers of an early-afternoon sun. Nothing was to be seen except two geese. Then I saw something more surprising: at the foot of a tree were two chairs, a table, and a picnic hamper. Paul smiled at my amazement. "My crew know where we stop for lunch. They come out in the Jeep and leave everything here. They will be back later to take it away." Midway through our meal Paul stopped suddenly and stood up. "Did you hear that? Buffalo grunts. We should stay quiet for a while." I had heard nothing. A little later he asked me if I had caught the sound of an elephant scream. I had heard nothing.

We carried on for some hours after lunch down the hunter's track. Just before reaching base camp we sighted some elephant on the other side of a gully. As we stood watching them, one suddenly appeared on our side of the gully. Ears outstretched, trunk curled in our direction, it charged without warning. "Run! Run!" We tore through the bush, scrambling away as fast as we could from three tons of animal headed in our direction with two needle-sharp tusks ready to run us through. We had gone perhaps a hundred yards when the elephant decided we were not worth the bother. He slowed to a halt and trumpeted his superiority.

"What would you have done if he had continued his charge?" I asked Paul in between breaths.

"I would have fired a shot in the air. That usually puts them to flight. If he had continued, then I would have had to shoot."

By the end of that first day, my sight and hearing were keener than I had ever known. I was learning to respect the natural world not just as an idea but as objective fact that I disregarded at my peril. I realized, reflecting in my tent that evening, how much of my attention was bound up in subjective experience. Paul Oliver, by contrast, had given a great deal of his time and attention to observing the world about him. In doing so, he had given rise to an unsentimental love of the wild, and a genuine wish to protect it.

He told me over dinner that evening why he had chosen to site his camp just outside the national park. The migration routes were being threatened by a rapid development in cash-crop farming. Speculators from Dar es Salaam were buying up land to grow beans, a major staple in East Africa that could yield up to three harvests a year. After months of delicate negotiations with the local Masai and the government, Paul was able to secure the protection of thousands of acres outside the park, thus keeping the migration routes open. The presence of his camp in the protected area helps to ensure that the agreement is honored, and is also a deterrent to hunters and poachers.

Poaching is still an international trade in Africa. Thirty years ago there were half a million elephants in Tanzania. In 1996 there were an estimated thirty-five thousand. The ivory ban, which came into effect in 1989, has dramatically slowed the fall in numbers, but there is a strong lobby to have the ban lifted. In 1986 the number of elephants killed to supply the U.S. market for worked ivory amounted to 32,254; and seventy-five percent of that year's imports originated from African countries that had prohibited ivory exports. Nez Percé chief Seattle's words, spoken in America toward the close of the nineteenth century, ring as a somber warning at the dawn of the millennium:

"What happens to beasts will happen to man. All things are connected. If the great beasts are gone, man would surely die of a great loneliness of spirit."

We walked for hours the next day on the edge of the park, through grass that often swayed above our heads. I have never been so aware of where I was putting my feet. My head has never swiveled so diligently to scan a horizon. But we had no cause for alarm that day. We saw several pairs of lovebirds——green parrots that always fly with their mates——and often walked within range of a go-away bird (the sound of their call gives them their name). Zebra, giraffe, impala, the fringe-eared oryx often ran in file across our path.

"We know so much about the natural world," Paul commented as we watched some zebra grazing in the distance, "but some of the most commonly known facts still hold a mystery. Everyone knows the zebra has

stripes, for example, but no one has yet been able to satisfactorily explain why."

In the early afternoon Paul suddenly motioned to me to stop. He had caught sight of a wildebeest. "If we wait here a few moments, we may see a herd of them on their way back into the park." Sure enough, they came by soon after he had spoken, perhaps a hundred of them in single file, moving fast and intently just twenty yards ahead of us. I had not known until then that these curiously graceful creatures, which looked to me like a cross between a striped horse and a buffalo, were also known as gnus. The gnu, in my imagination, had always been a mythical creature, a sort of hybrid fantasy that one encounters in children's stories. Now here I was marveling at the reality. Hundreds of thousands of them are born every year on the edge of the Serengeti, though only a small percentage escape the lions' jaws. Wildebeest and buffalo, Paul informed me, diverged on different branches of the Bovidae family of mammals 4 to 5 million years ago. Cattle evolved from another branch of the same family.

Toward the end of the day we went down into a gully where there were still a few traces of water. We moved slowly, eyes everywhere. Even so, we surprised a lone buffalo. He was an elderly male, perhaps fifteen years old, who could no longer keep up with the herd. He ran as soon as he saw us. "Being alone makes him vulnerable," said Paul. "He's nervous. He knows he will end up as lion meat eventually."

That night we slept out on a rock that gave us a view of the African land to a far horizon. We could see beyond the green swamp into the park in one direction, and as far as Mount Meru and Kilimanjaro in another. The great plains of grass and acacia stretched away behind us to the west. Next to us on a ledge of the rock was a hyena lair, littered with bones.

I was beginning to realize how Africa is a primordial world, not just of tooth and claw but of delicate balance, of fine-tuned relations of one species with another: cunning, stealth, skillful avoidance, respect, attention generate an instinctive nobility there.

On my last day we walked for hours under a hot sun toward a water hole where we would spend the night.

In the early afternoon we were trudging through high grass with a gully on our left and a long ridge beyond it. Ahead, some five hundred yards, were a herd of wildebeest and zebra in a line that pointed toward the gully. Two wildebeest at the head of the line were edging nervously toward the gully. The others were watching them keenly.

"The gully is where the cats wait for a kill," Paul said as we crept a little closer. "This is one of the migration routes back into the park. Now that the rains have finished, there is little water to be had except along the Tarangire River, in the park. They will be coming through here in the hundreds in the next few weeks. There's probably a cat down there now."

Suddenly the leading wildebeest came racing back from the gully, and the whole herd clustered together. Then I see it, the head of a female lion peering above the grasses before the gully. The potential prey are all erect, necks craned toward the lion, with an occasional glance at us.

"The lion has to get within twenty yards or it doesn't stand a chance," said Paul. "The zebra and wildebeest can easily outstrip her over a distance. The forces of evolution have calibrated everything here to a fine balance. In fact the lion is successful only once in every five or six attempts at a kill, except when the prey has young."

The wildebeest, after twenty minutes or so of indecision, finally led the zebra off on another route through the gully. The lion turned to gaze at a distant giraffe, looked across at us, and lowered itself back into the grass for another wait.

We reached the water hole just before sunset. Two tents had been pitched, and a table stood between them. Buffalo were grunting in the trees. Two zebra faded from view. Then, as we sat there, silent in the dusk, twenty to thirty elephants with their young emerged without a sound from the trees on the far side. Trunks in the air, ears stretched out, they moved forward a step at a time toward the water. I sat there in awe at the grace and power of these huge creatures, who can walk on the tips of their toes in silence and can sprint at thirty to forty miles an hour, who can pick up a pin or remove a thorn with their trunk, or stun a dog with a single sneeze.

"The beast that passeth all others in wit and mind . . . and by its intellect makes as near an approach to man as matter can approach spirit," wrote Lucretius in *De Rerum Natura*.

Today it is more fashionable to speak of dolphins or whales in the terms that Lucretius used. Yet these creatures slipping toward me now through the shadows, they cry salt tears when in distress. They mourn their dead; they greet one another by touching their trunks to one another's foreheads; they communicate like whales, it has recently been discovered, with subsonic calls—which explains why herds in different places often move in orchestrated patterns.

Even when they reached the edge and began drinking, there was hardly a sound that came to us across the water. They had been there only a few minutes when a herd of zebra came flitting through the grass. Paul explained in a whisper that they always waited for the elephant to warn of any danger first before going down to the water.

I was filled with the utter beauty and economy of the scene. No movement seemed to be without a purpose, and none lasted longer than was necessary. The half-moon rising gave a glow to the water and caught the outlines of more zebra coming down to replace those who had already taken water. The elephant began to make off through the acacias to our left; as they did so, a family of buffalo came crashing out of the undergrowth and jostled the zebra, grunting and snorting down the water in gulps.

As the rest of the elephants merged noiselessly with the trees, two bulls stayed behind, a hundred yards to our left, to engage in a tusk joust. Their silhouettes were traced by the moon, their ivory gleamed in the half-light. The thwack of tusk against tusk rang through the night air. The buffalo were lowing, coughing, splashing. Eventually one elephant broke away and headed in the direction of the herd. The other bull returned to the water hole and back the other way. It had just been beaten in a duel for the female head of the herd and would have to seek out another mate. Somewhere an elephant trumpeted, and another responded from farther away in the trees. We sat there, in the place where the world began, while the moon traveled far and we never noticed.

That night in my tent I awoke to a lion's roar. Stay in the tent; even if something brushes up against it, you'll be safe, Paul had said. Though our scent is on the wind, they can't quite fathom where we are; the tent is another bush to them. Elephants trumpeted, hyenas barked that night, and I was glad—so glad that I slept more briefly and deeply than I have ever done. And I understood in those few night hours why people like Paul Oliver had committed their lives to being out here in the wilderness of Africa. There, by that water hole, we were part of the great hierarchy of nature again. We belonged, we were unequivocally alive, and it was impossible not to respect and admire the life in every other thing.

Rumi:
Turning *for* Love

*A lover may hanker after this or that love
But at the last he is drawn to the King of love.
However much we describe and explain love
When we fall in love we are ashamed of our words.
Explanation by the tongue makes most things clear,
But love unexplained is clearer.*

— J A L A L   A L - D I N   R U M I

What else could I call this life whose threads have been running through my fingers, if not a lover's journey? Who else but a madman would run all over the earth looking for what he knows he already has? Though in the verse above he warns against speaking of love, no one is more eloquent about it than Jalal al-Din Rumi:

"What is unification? To burn oneself before the One."

Seven hundred years after his death in Konya, Turkey, it seems almost as though his poems are read in America more than the work of any other poet. All those lovers looking for home, yet we already recognize somehow the delight of being there. Rumi was the founder of the Mevlevi (Whirling Dervishes) in Konya in the thirteenth century. He was a brilliant scholar and theologian with a large following when his life was burnt to a cinder one day by his meeting with a wandering dervish, Shams of Tabriz. In and through

Shams he encountered the One True Friend, threw all his books away, and began to dance in the ecstasy of love. The dance ceremony (*sama'*) still performed today by the members of his order is a formalization of that original joy.

There is a picture on my study wall of Rumi sitting absorbed in prayer. It has watched over me for fifteen years. Though I went once with my son to Konya when he was barely into his teens, I had never attended the *'urs*, the dance ceremony in December that commemorates Rumi's death, his wedding with the Lord. Then, one day in the summer of 1996, I mentioned my interest to a friend in Germany who was the disciple of a Sufi master living in Istanbul.

"Why don't you go with him?" she said. "He is taking a group of disciples on a pilgrimage round the shrines of the saints in Anatolia, and they will stay a few days in Konya for the *'urs*. Far better to go with an authority like him who can lead you to people and places you might never get to know on your own."

I had voiced a desire, and life had opened the door. I was not used to traveling in a group, or having someone else lead the way, though this was how pilgrims had traveled the world over for millennia. The timing, the synchronicity, seemed to point the way, though I remembered how the same had been true for Sedona, where, in the event, I stayed for just two days before heading out to Big Sur in California. You just never know, so better to do it anyway, I thought. But there was more to the equation than Rumi. My friend had spoken to me several times about her Sufi *shaikh*—how he was a master of ancient music, an ethnomusicologist at Istanbul University who had collected Sufi music from all over Central Asia and was recognized as a *shaikh* by three different Sufi orders, of whom the Mevlevi, Rumi's order, was one. His name was Oruç Gevenç. I had intended to meet him on a few occasions before, but for one reason or another it had never happened. Now, it seemed, was the time.

"Go to the music shop in the main street of Sultanahmet. It belongs to the brother of Uruch, and he will explain where to meet us." Those were the only joining instructions I received. I made a hotel reservation from London and let the organizers of the party know where I would be. When I arrived, just before midnight, there was a message telling me to come to a hotel nearby the next morning, when the group would be leaving early for Edirne, near the Bulgarian border.

In the morning I awoke to find another message: they were not going to Edirne after all, but would meet later in the day to visit the shrine of a saint in Istanbul. The old Sufi tactics, I thought, everything changing at a moment's notice; dislocate the linear mind, its need for control. I've signed up, so I go with it. At the appointed time I strolled through the streets of Sultanahmet, behind the church-museum of Hagia Sophia, over to the other hotel. In the dining room twenty or so Europeans, mostly Spanish and Austrian, were talking over coffee. Fatima, the Austrian organizer I had talked to on the phone, greeted me more like an old friend than a first acquaintance, and proceeded to tell me that Uruch had been held up, but that "he won't be long."

Almost everyone else in the room had worked with Uruch before, learning to play the instruments—the *ney,* the *rabat,* the *ud*—that were used in Sufi music and learning the Sufi dances. Several had been on solitary personal retreats under his guidance, a few for as long as forty days. Michaela Ozelsel, the friend who had first told me of Uruch, had written a book on her experience of the forty-day *halvet,* or solitary retreat, that had become a bestseller in Germany. The group was mostly women—a designer, an artist, a marketing consultant from Vienna, the curator of a museum in Barcelona, a teacher, a chef who ran the kitchen of a five-star hotel in Bavaria, and an Iranian woman who worked for the government tourist office in Tehran. There was a man who taught the guitar, another who ran his own retail business, and a couple who ran a home for the mentally disturbed in a remote corner of Austria. There were no Turks. Uruch, it appeared, spent most of his time teaching in Europe.

Two hours later Fatima came into the room to announce that Uruch had arrived and we were ready to go. In the hotel doorway stood a tiny man of about fifty with a shock of gray hair, dressed in a blue suit and tie, with black shoes polished to perfection. Uruch had been born a hunchback and walked with a painful limp. On his face, however, was the smile of a child, wide-eyed and open. He greeted everyone in turn, apologized for the delay (perhaps it wasn't a "teaching" after all), and led us to our bus.

No Blue Mosque or Topkapi Palace museum on this tour. No, we were

off to the tomb of Eyyub Sultan, Mohammed's standard-bearer and one of
his relations. The tomb of a Muslim saint is usually attached to a mosque,
and the complex built in honor of Eyyub was magnificent, fifteenth-century
Ottoman. Uruch said a short prayer in front of the tomb, and while I stood
gazing in admiration at the tile work on the outer wall of the building, he led
most of his disciples down a side alley to sacrifice a goat in honor of two who
had just taken Muslim names. My God, I thought, we are still in the time of
Abraham. Yet animal sacrifice, I came to learn, is deeply ingrained in Islam,

and even a man of culture such as Uruch honored the tradition. The sacrificial meat is given away to the poor and is considered especially holy.

People, mostly women, filed past me into the building that housed the tomb, pausing here and there to kiss the wall. Two old men were absorbed in their ablutions at a fountain by the door. Inside, families were sitting quietly at prayer on the floor in front of a tomb draped with a green silk cloth. The silence was palpable. Here and there men sat on their own, immersed in the Koran. I had seen this devotion to the saints in India, where, as in the Muslim and Christian worlds, they are revered for the blessings they can bestow and for the healings that occur at their shrines. There was a presence in the shrine of Eyyub that I was grateful for, and I was glad to have stayed there on my own rather than followed the rest to the sacrifice.

The goat's blood was quickly spilled; in fifteen minutes the party had returned and we were ready to go on to the tomb of Yusu, who lay in state outside the city on a hill overlooking the Bosporus. Yusu, Fatima told me as we puttered through the traffic and over the bridge into Asian Istanbul, was the biblical Joshua. Muslims know that Joshua was an Israelite, that there is no record of his ever having traveled to Turkey, but that counts for little when several great Sufi *shaikh*s have all dreamt that he was born on this hill outside of Istanbul. There is circumstantial evidence too: the flocks of successive shepherds have always refused to graze in that spot, always a sign of some special event. Anyway, Fatima explained, if those who can see into other dimensions say that something is so, then it is so.

It must be a tomb of unusual attraction, I thought, with all this effort to pay our respects to it. We had been driving for a couple of hours already, and still no hint of this hill. We wound along the shore, past great villas with their own jetties onto the water, through far-flung suburbs, until eventually, with the sun low in the sky, we climbed through wooded hills to stop at last on a crest with a spectacular view of the Bosporus and the Black Sea beyond. Through a gate we went, and there it was, an unusually long rectangle of earth, waist high, held in place by stone walls, open to the sky and the straits far below.

I stood there trying to feel something, trying to enter into some sympathetic communion with this Old Testament prophet whom Islam had appropriated for its own. All I could register was the dying light on the water below, the sun dipping below the hills, the wind lifting softly through the trees. The view was worth coming for. But from the rectangle of turf, well, nothing. Uruch went to the trinket shop nearby and bought a fistful of rosaries, each with thirty-three beads, one-third of the ninety-nine names of God (the hundredth name, being invisible and inaudible, can't be told). Rubbing them first with a dash of musk, the scent most beloved of Mohammed, he handed us one each with a murmured blessing, and we piled back into the bus for the journey home.

The next day we did go to Edirne, a few hours north, near the borders of Greece and Bulgaria. Uruch led the way in his car, while the rest of us followed in the bus.

"Our journeys are caravans, caravans of dreams," Fatima told me. "It would be more logical for everyone to travel in the same vehicle, since there is room enough, but with two or more cars we create a sense of community, one car always having to look out for the other. Music and friendship, these are the essence of Sufism."

Edirne is a beautiful town with an ancient history, its mosque one of the finest in Turkey, but we were not there for sightseeing. Our sole objective was to visit the building that for five hundred years, until the end of the nineteenth century, had been a music therapy and healing center. Empty now, it was under the jurisdiction of the local university, which had just invited

Uruch to revive its original function there. Uruch led a music group in Istanbul called Tumata, which was well known for its research into traditional healing music from all over Central Asia.

On the edge of town, along a dirt road by the canal, we stopped outside a magnificent building with arches leading through enclosed courtyards, dozens of small domes, and one main cupola. The entire place was empty. We stopped under the main cupola. Uruch sat on a platform to one side of the dome and took out his *ud*, a kind of lute that has been used in the Orient for centuries. The musicians would sit on these platforms, he explained, and minister to the mentally sick who were brought here from all over the region. Then he began to minister to us. The notes spread softly around the dome, and he began to sing with such a plaintive tenderness that in minutes half the group were weeping.

Eyes closed, my mind beginning to float away on the lilt of his voice, I became vaguely aware of the ring of a telephone. Looking around for the source of the irritant, I noticed Uruch fumbling in his waistcoat, singing all the while and playing his *ud* now with one hand. His fingers came out of his waistcoat clutching a cell phone, and he began holding a low conversation with someone while continuing to play. The interruption seemed to make little difference to the mood of the group, and I was truly impressed with the way Uruch seemed able to carry on two seemingly incompatible activities at the same time. Over the following ten days I was to witness many examples of his capacity for split attention, since his cell phone was never silent for long. Sometimes he would deliberately break a mood with its opposite, throwing his instrument in the air or swiveling his hat round on his head just when the atmosphere was getting too serious.

That evening, back in Istanbul, we were invited to a formal celebration of the twentieth anniversary of Tumata. Two hundred people were crammed into a room near Uruch's brother's shop; a government official opened the proceedings with some formal introductions; and various musicians stood to give votes of thanks. The thanks and the counterthanks went on for hours, audible testimony to the Oriental love of protocol and respect. Everyone's name had to be honored, and whenever a soloist got to his or her feet, he or she was invariably begged to offer a song. Eventually, Uruch spoke, thanking his family, introducing them all, and ending with another heartrending melody on his *ud*. Sometime after midnight the cloths were lifted from a huge table of food, and everyone set to with the hummus and halvah while I spoke to Rafik, a translator of Sufi poetry and one of the few locals who could speak English.

"There are practically no real Sufis left now," he began by saying. "We live in a different time. Istanbul is as Western as any European city, and we have to adapt the language and essence of Sufism to the present climate. Uruch is one of the few who has had a genuine training. He lived in the house of one of his masters for at least a year, barely going out, absorbed in the inner work, being graced with many spontaneous psychic capabilities. He has taken Sufism to the West through his music, and is giving it a different form there, more open, less authoritarian, with no segregation between men and women, both of whom are regarded equally. Yet in many ways he is still a traditionalist, and his closest disciples tend to convert to Islam. For myself, I am convinced that we have to step beyond these religious distinctions now. True spirituality is not about religion, though it is not easy to make the distinction in the case of Sufism, which is so inextricably bound up with Islam."

Just then, the music started up again, but I had taken in enough for one day. With a shake of Rafik's hand I went back to the hotel for a few hours of sleep. We headed out in the morning in three vehicles, Uruch's brother having lent us his van for the baggage. I had heard we were aiming to be in Bursa that night, but for the rest, unknown.

"The whole point of this kind of journey," said Fatima as we raced down the freeway, Uruch in the lead in his Fiat, "is *suchurat*. It means accept, and defend nothing. Whatever comes, comes. And all this time in the bus, doing nothing, it's important. There can be a thin line between boredom and deeper levels, just like in the recitations, when you might be saying the same phrase over and over for hours, bored out of your brain, apparently not connected to the meaning of the words at all, then *wham!* something hits you in between one phrase and the next, you wake up, and you realize why you have been doing this stupid practice all these hours."

Thank God for Fatima, I thought, she will keep me in line. She was also one of the only members of the group who spoke good English, having lived a married life in Wisconsin for five years in an earlier incarnation. She had first met Uruch ten years previously and had followed his way ever since. She, her new husband, and another couple organized Uruch's European program from a center they had begun outside of Vienna. They called it the Academy for Traditional Central Asian and Turkish Music, which wasn't so strange, because there had been a similar institution outside of Vienna during the Ottoman period.

We left the freeway after an hour or two and went down to a ferry that hauled us across the Bosporus to the shore. The province of Bursa—I knew from my map—faced the sea an hour or two down the coast. Within thirty kilometers or so of the city of the same name, however, we turned suddenly off the main road in the direction of a place called Iznik. I was beginning not to care about destinations. Fatima was right: this meandering, wandering route was taking me into dream time, to a permeable, receptive condition where perhaps I might hear voices other than my own, or simply fall asleep. Every so often we would all stop so that Uruch could take notes from a phone call.

Along a lake of long shadows and rose sky we drove, on and on, till sometime after nightfall we stopped in a small town by the lakeshore. *Iznik*, said the sign; and under that, *Nicaea*. We stood in a huddle beneath the city walls while Uruch explained that this was indeed the site of the ancient city of Nicaea, where two ecclesiastical councils were held—one in 325, the second in 787—to determine the Christian tenets of faith and which books would compose the New Testament.

We followed him through the old city gate, down a backstreet, and there by a corner was the shrine of Esrefolgu Abdullah Rumi, a fifteenth-century Sufi poet (not to be confused with Rumi of Konya), educated by some of the best-known scholars of the period and founder of a branch of the Qadiri Sufis. Five minutes in a light drizzle, Uruch leading a short chant, *"Bismillah—Irrahman—Irrahim . . ."* Then back to the bus for the drive to Bursa, and a stop in a roadside café for dinner, which should not, Uruch advised us, include spinach, potatoes, tomatoes, fish, pork, chocolate, or coffee. "These foods forbidden in our tradition," he explained. "So please, for the journey, not these foods." It seemed an odd mix to avoid, though most of the items were acidic. Another case of direct knowledge from a level transcending logic? I wondered, half amused. Anyway, just another opportunity to accept the situation for what it was. I was beginning to find a certain satisfaction in just following along.

In the bus I picked up something from the others about the Sufi Esrefolgu. He was, I was told, one of the first people to write poetry in Turkish. From a family of generations of Sufis himself, he met a *shaikh* one day whose permanent state of ecstasy impressed him deeply. But I need a sign, he thought to himself, to know that he is really my *shaikh*.

The master asked him to go and fetch a bowl of soup for him with two *kofta* (meat) balls. Esrefolgu went off and found the soup, but not the *kofta*. "Where is the *kofta*?" the master asked.

"I couldn't find any," Esrefolgu replied.

The master took two pebbles, dropped them in the soup, and they became *kofta*. So faith can achieve anything. Faith isn't, I pondered, a question of blind belief; it's an imaginative leap, a willingness to conceive that with a shift of mind the world itself turns on a different axis. It is imagination that is in short supply, not belief. The Iranian woman commented that she had witnessed Kurdish Sufis in Iran plunge knives down into their skulls and through their cheeks while dancing in front of their master. When the knives were pulled out the wounds healed instantly with not a drop of blood spilt.

Esrefolgu's master later sent him on to other *shaikh*s, including Hajji Bayran Veli of Ankara, in whose *tekke* (Sufi community) he stayed for eleven years. During that time he did all the menial work for the community and was permitted to speak to the *shaikh* only once a year. Hajji Bayran eventually sent him on to Hamevi, another great saint of the period, who gave him his daughter in marriage and sent him into *halvet,* the forty-day solitary retreat. For the last part Esrefolgu stopped eating, drinking, and sleeping. The other disciples thought he was dead; then the *shaikh* whispered three times in his ear, "Wake up!"

"Oh, you are cutting my heart, Master!"

"But the world needs you, you cannot stay in this state."

So Sufi, this: that any grace or illumination you receive is for the benefit of the world at large.

It was quite late in the evening when we rolled into Bursa. Instead of going to a hotel we stopped outside a high-walled garden in the old part of town. Uruch knocked on the green door. It was opened by a short bearded man wearing a green fez who greeted us with a slight bow, right arm folded across his heart. In the middle of the garden was an old timber house, front door open, ready to receive us. By the door stood a distinguished-looking man, tall, fine-featured, and bearded, wearing old corduroys, woolly cardigan, and slippers. He was, we gathered, the *shaikh* of one of the three *tekke*s still surviving in Bursa, and this, his house, had served as a *tekke* for three hundred years. His family had provided the *shaikh*s of the order for generations, and the tombs of his father and grandfather, both *shaikh*s before him, were in the garden.

We filed into a room with an old stove in the middle and beautiful calligraphy around the walls. In one corner was a white marble fountain. A couple of young men busied themselves making black tea and handing it round in little glasses. The two *shaikh*s sat down next to each other, and with a certain formality our host made us welcome, giving a lengthy speech and paying his respects to Uruch. Uruch then replied with another speech. All due honor was paid to everyone present, and finally, the music began. Uruch brought out the *ney* this time, a bamboo flute that evokes more than any instrument I can think of the longing of the soul for its Beloved. The *shaikh* instructed the man with the fez to sing, which he did with a passion that cut to the quick. What a way to live a life, I reflected, given to that love so entirely.

On and on it went, with first one, then another person leading the *zikr*, the recitation of God's name, head turning one way with the in breath, the other with the out breath, faster and faster, slower again, quietly, then the words pushed out like ejaculations. Two of the Spaniards fell on the floor in tears, the arms of another jerking involuntarily. The two *shaikh*s all the while were sitting in elegant composure, chanting softly. When the time had run its course, Uruch quietly put his instruments away and signaled an end to the evening.

Back in the bus I noticed it was past two in the morning. We drove to the center of town and stopped while Uruch ran about looking for a hotel to take twenty-five people. "Why didn't you book a hotel?" I asked Kadir with evident irritation. Kadir was Uruch's first assistant and driver of one of the vans.

"We want to be free to take things as they come," he replied. "There won't be a problem, it's just a matter of faith."

"Well, there's a Sufi saying that I've always found useful," I retorted, "and that is, 'Trust in God, but tie your camel.'"

We waited in the bus until Uruch and Kadir, turned down by several places, finally found two that could take us between them. I fell at last into bed, to be awoken (it seemed like five minutes later) at 8 A.M. by a loud knock at the door. Uruch was about to give a talk in the lobby on some of the saints whose shrines we were going to visit today in Bursa. I've heard that one before, I thought; he won't be giving any talk for ages. I fell asleep again, to be awoken a little while later by someone who seemed intent on breaking the door in.

Muttering under my breath, I struggled into my clothes and went down to the lobby, to find everyone already sitting there and Uruch in full flight. I snatched a glass of tea and sat down.

"'I have left the colors of the world behind me,'" he was reading from some book. "'I have accepted the colors of love, joined love's caravan. Belief and nonbelief have blown away. The ocean has overcome me. The eight heavens and the seven hells do not understand me anymore, because Allah, the Lord, is calling me. Why try to make an imperfect world more beautiful? I have made my contract with the Beloved. This is why I am drunk. I am putting all matters of this world into the cup of love, and I offer my life to the joy of having arrived.'"

What a way to wake up. I was suddenly grateful to whoever had been hitting my door.

"That was Eftade," Uruch went on, "a great saint who lived in Bursa. Before his birth his mother dreamt of a child swimming in a milk ocean. That meant he would be one of the knowing ones. Eftade had a wonderful voice and people would pay him to sing. One night he had a dream and a voice said, 'You will fall from the Lord's staircase by accepting money for his gift to you.' He gave all his money away and devoted his life to Allah. He was the founder of the Jelveti order. We will visit his tomb."

In due course off we went round the tombs of Bursa, led by Uruch and the *shaikh* we had met the night before. Which tomb was which I gave up trying to remember, tombs coming out of my ears already, and this only a day or two into the journey. It didn't really matter anyway; it was the wandering that counted, the wandering in a different dimension from that of the Bursa that lay all around us, the chic, elegant city that had been the first capital of the Ottoman Empire and that now sported cappuccino bars and fashion accessory shops on every corner. And we, a motley band of Europeans, traipsing round from tomb to tomb down one backstreet after another, drinking in tales of saints who had lived five hundred years before.

I remember the shoemaker's tomb, the one who flew to Mecca and back in three days on the wings of grace. His story makes him difficult to forget. His main disciple was the city judge, who was willing to sell goat stomachs in the market if that was what his master wanted of him. When the *shaikh* saw his willingness to forgo his rank, he said the judge could remain in his post, for there were all too few with his virtues in such a position.

Then there was the hall that housed a saint, his wife, and their several sons, their tombs all draped in fine white lace. I sat there for an age, it seemed, with Fatima falling into a trance beside me. She was so absorbed I left her in her delight to follow the rest, who had gone off to pay their respects to someone else. Outside the hall an old man was pulling vigorously at his ears as he sat on a marble stool by the ablutions fountain. Then he scrubbed his hands and feet in readiness for afternoon prayers.

Outside the main mosque of the city is a tomb that Uruch had seen in a dream before ever coming to Bursa. He was told it was the tomb of Hajji Bey, another fifteenth-century master. Later, on his first visit to the city, he discovered his dream was correct. Dreams and visions play a large part in the Sufi tradition. Uruch told me that for him the only real knowledge was that of intuition, the kind that comes through direct perception. The most precise knowledge of all, one of his teachers had said, was love. Everything else was dream.

That night we returned to the *tekke* of the Bursa *shaikh*. More *zikrs* were sung, talks were given, there were readings from holy scripture. An incredible sense of community and Old World courtesy. Uruch's two daughters had joined us in Bursa, and at one point, while their father was in the middle of some explanation, one of them, a ten-year-old, went over to him and started rearranging his hair. All the while she fiddled with his parting and tried to make his hair go the other way, pushing his head this way and that, he carried on speaking as if nothing was happening. I had never seen such consideration for the different levels of reality. Fatima told me later that Sufis pay great attention to what children do. They let them play as they like, looking for signs, noticing which book they pick up or where they open it, because children are close still to the angelic realms.

Everything matters for the Sufis. When our host had finished reading to us, he kissed the book before closing it. His disciples kissed the table we ate on, and when the time came to take photographs, the *shaikh* even kissed his camera. When leaving the presence of a *shaikh,* Sufis back out of the room, turning away from the *shaikh* only when they reach the door. All this in the heart of a city that was as materialistic and image conscious as any in the West. We were in a tiny oasis that lived by the values of a vanishing world. This *shaikh* was the last of his line, and he lived in the *tekke* alone with his mother. He was dedicating his time to renovating the *tekke* to its original form, and when I asked him about his own teacher, he said, "You know, I understand very little about anything except wooden houses. I am a restorer of old timber buildings, that is all."

Before we left he took us upstairs to see the *sema* (dance) room, which took up the whole of the top floor. Generations of Sufis had turned in ecstasy in this room, their *shaikh* watching over them from a raised dais at one end. The names of Allah were inscribed on the walls from floor to ceiling in calligraphy. Downstairs, he showed me his father's calligraphy tools, kept in a school pencil case that must have been bought in the fifties. They use the *sema* room only on the five holy nights of the year now, he said.

We parted that night as late as we had the night before, with more warmth and kindness than I can remember. "We have a long way to go tomorrow," said Uruch as we were leaving, "so we should be on our way by six." That was in about three hours' time. I was just about to fall into my anxiety about sleep——not having enough of it——when suddenly I realized I wasn't tired. Then I saw what I had never seen before: this concern, it is fear at the root, fear of illness, and ultimately of death. My fear of death was driving my need for sleep——it came to me not as a deduction but as a lightning flash that lit up my view of myself. As soon as I saw it a heaviness lifted, joy burst in.

At five the hotelier was knocking at my door. Sometime before then I was awoken bolt upright by a brief sharp call——"*Allah!*"——that came from neither inside nor outside of me. God is great, that's all I know.

We took off for Ankara through strands of mist; the day seemed to grow darker with each passing hour. By the early afternoon we had reached our first stop, the tomb of Hajji Bayran Veli in Ankara, a popular place for the locals, who were lined up in pouring rain, newspapers on their heads, to beg favors of their city's saint. The cupola above his shrine was decorated with a thousand roses. Uruch whispered that the rose was the symbol of divine intimacy and presence. We sang a chant, stayed half an hour, and continued on our way to Kirsehir, one of the vans breaking down just five kilometers from the town. What did it matter? We weren't going anywhere in particular, just round and round. I smiled at myself, aware of how different this was from my usual reaction to delay. We fiddled under the hood for a while to no avail, and finally left the van by the road for the night and continued with the other vehicles into Kirsehir, where we fell into a hotel oppo-

site the shrine of Ahi Evran. That night Uruch sang the songs of Hajji Bayran, and I marveled to see the young waiters mouth the words along with him. The last words he said that night were, "The soul is a caravan, life a hotel. We stop by and leave. Good night."

Before leaving, of course, we had to pay Ahi Evran a call. Like many of the other saints whose shrines we had visited, he had come to Anatolia from Central Asia on the instruction of a dream. He was a leather worker and one of the principal figures to connect Sufism with the practice of a craft and work in the world. Though they withdraw for periodic solitary retreats, the Sufis are not usually renunciates. Their practice takes place in the heart of everyday life. Ahi Evran founded the first guild system, in the thirteenth century, and the point of his guild was to ensure that tradesmen worked according to ethical principles. What that meant in his time was that if a customer went down a row of leather shops in the bazaar and stopped to buy something, the shopkeeper might say, "Go down to my neighbor. He hasn't sold anything all day."

His shrine was a small domed building on some open ground, and in this one I felt at home as soon as I entered. A gathered presence somehow in this simple space with faded carpets on the floor, a stone turban at the head of the tomb, and the roses, all those roses again, in a lattice over the ceiling, and the scent of rose water. I sat there until someone came to tell me the other van had arrived and we were ready to head on to Konya.

We stopped at one more tomb that day, whose owner was the first saint I had heard of. Hajji Bektash Vali ("hajji" meaning one who has completed the hajj, or pilgrimage to Mecca) was another Sufi who, like Ahi Evran, came to Anatolia from Khorasan in Central Asia. I knew of him because he was the founder of a famous Sufi order, the Bektashi dervishes. He was apparently told to bring the teachings to Anatolia by a shaman, and his order still practices a synthesis of Central Asian shamanistic practices and Islam. His tomb is in a tiny village in central Anatolia and is part of a complex that served as his *tekke* in the fifteenth century.

Through a low door to the side of the main hall was the tiny room with no window where Bektash himself performed his *halvet*, the air so still in there that it seemed to draw everyone to the ground. In the main hall, Uruch began playing his *ud* and motioned to some of the group to begin a dance that he said was an ancient Bektashi one. In a circle all together they went; on their own they turned, hands crossed over the chest; in pairs they bowed in honor of each other. I felt I was standing in a waterfall—these tombs, I realized all of a sudden, being fountains of energy, gateways between this world and another, connecting nodes, across space and time, all round the globe, of all traditions.

We crawled into Konya through thick fog and reached the hotel soon after midnight. Drifting into the street from the lobby came a familiar refrain: *"L'a Illaha illalla . . ."* We opened the lobby door to be struck by a wave of sound, sixty or seventy people chanting at the top of their lungs. A row of men, arms linked, were bending their knees and rising up and down with the breath. At one end was a group of musicians next to a seated man who was looking round the room slowly, nodding his head. The linked men were smiling, bellies rising and falling like bellows. As we came in, those who were sitting, including a dozen smartly dressed women, rose to their feet and joined the men, and everyone began circling the lobby, almost competing with one another to exhale the most forcefully. I had never seen such an ecstatic sight in a hotel in all my life.

One of the men, a look of pure devotion on his face, broke free of the circle and bowed before the elderly man, moving his hands from his heart out in a gesture of open welcome over and over again, his head moving from one side to the other as he continued to sing the name of Allah along with everyone else. Then a woman joined him and broke out in her own song above the general chorus, pouring her heart out to her *shaikh*.

When their *shaikh* caught sight of Uruch, he beckoned him over to a seat next to him; the music subsided, and the two men exchanged a few words of greeting. Uruch took his *ud* from its case and began playing, and our group joined with the other in the first lines of the Koran, *"Bismillah—Irrahman—Irrahim . . ."* In the name of God, the most gracious and merciful . . .

The bellow breathing started up again. Everyone joined hands, circling the lobby, the hotel staff oblivious, our luggage still in the van. For hours first one *shaikh* then another led the music, each commanding now and then his principal disciple to whirl, arms outstretched, before him and the rest of the assembly. Sometime after three the night finally ended with a speech from each *shaikh* paying his respects to the other.

A few hours later I was outside the tomb of Shams of Tabriz, before the tourist rush had begun. Konya was packed that week with Sufi groups, tourists, and busloads of the devout from the countryside who had descended on the town for the *'urs*, whose main attraction was the performance of the Whirling Dervish dance, the *sema*, in the local sports hall.

I had rather surprised myself by rising early to go to another tomb, but this was, after all, the resting place of Shams, immortalized in Rumi's poetry. Shams was a member of the Qalandar order, who take only the lowest stations in life and give service. His great sadness was that he had no true spiritual friend with whom to share his deepest thoughts. He begged Allah to let him meet someone with whom he could speak. "There is someone in Konya," Allah replied. "If I let you meet him, what will you give me in return?"

"My head," replied Shams.

"Granted. His name is Rumi."

When the two met, their hearts were changed forever. Rumi's disciples were so jealous of their master's love for this unknown vagrant, however, that they killed him. The pain that the murder inflicted on Rumi resulted in some of the finest poetry the world has ever heard.

At the entrance to the tomb of Shams I saw someone I recognized, a woman I had not seen for fifteen years. She was with an English group of Sufis. As we embraced she said, laughing, "Are you still seeking, Roger?" I didn't know what to say.

I rejoined my group later in the day to take our afternoon seats at the sports hall. The *sema* has been officially banned since the early twenties, when Atatürk secularized the country and outlawed the Sufi orders, many of whom, including the Mevlevi, had become like small states within the state, with their own powers of jurisdiction over their members. I knew that the sports hall event was organized not by the Sufis but by the Ministry of Culture, that this was a tourist, not a spiritual occasion. We and the other Sufi groups in the audience were here for the symbolism of an event that had been held practically every year for centuries.

I was surprised, even so, to see the Coca-Cola advertisements all along the sports hall windows and to hear the drone of political speeches opening the event. The musicians who preceded the *sema* played with the grandiose gestures of television light opera. The *sema* was better served in London, I thought, where I had seen the dancers from Konya perform once at the Royal Albert Hall. At least there the surroundings were more fitting, sort of austerely gracious, and the audience, unfamiliar with the reality back in Turkey and thinking they were attending a spiritual ceremony, brought a respect to the gathering that did something to imbue it with dignity.

Here in the sports hall the dancers, in high felt hats and long white skirts, lined up in front of the *shaikh*, heads bowed, arms folded over their chest. The hats were their ego's tombstone, the skirt its shroud. The *ney* struck up its bittersweet tone, the Divine Breath breathing life into the dancers. Each of them peeled away from the line, bowed before the *shaikh*, began to turn on his axis around the hall, turning, turning around the heart, like the stars, the atoms, the blood in his veins, arms spread wide, right hand open to the sky to receive God's grace, left hand turned to the earth to pass the gift of grace on. Perhaps fifteen of them now, one or two of them boys still, some elderly men, turning for love, dissolving away before our eyes under the Coca-Cola signs. For half an hour or more they whirled along on their sacred journey, submitting their mind to the Perfect in love. This, at least, is the point of the *sema;* what went on behind those half-closed eyes we shall never know, though what matters to me is what was happening behind mine.

In front of me, on the other side of the hall, was a large white banner with the words of Rumi: *If you don't have any friend, why don't you find one? If you have found one, why don't you love him?* Every now and then throughout that turning dance, I prayed for that last line to burn in my heart.

That evening we were invited to the home of a retired dancer, one who had performed the *sema* for many years in Konya. The Mevlevi order had not been alive in the town for twenty years or more, he told us. Only in Istanbul are there circles who still retain the spirit of the work, with a genuine *shaikh*. Most dancers in Konya perform for their living now, rather than as a spiritual practice. When the dancer had talked for a while and the tea had come round, the zikr started up again.

Suddenly, in the middle of the chanting, Britta, the Austrian chef, let out a piercing scream and collapsed onto the person next to her. I shall never forget that scream. It was from somewhere else, from another realm altogether than this daylight one. Uruch continued playing, though every time he returned to a particular chord Britta let out a groan and writhed on the lap of her neighbor. When she eventually sat up there was a strange grin on her face and a drunken expression over which she clearly had no control. Every now and then she laughed wildly, placed her hands in a posture of prayer, and stood up to drape herself over Uruch. He responded as he might have done to a child, patting her head, continuing to sing as if nothing were happening.

Britta remained in this altered state for days, and I can only imagine what happened in her hotel kitchen on her return The rest of the group seemed in awe of her state and envied it as a visitation of grace. When I asked Uruch about it, he could only suggest that the experience of the journey was so radically different from her conventional Catholic upbringing that it had catalyzed an upsurge of unconscious material. He had plainly never encountered anything of the sort before.

Uruch was leaving for Istanbul the next day, along with Britta, whom he thought it best to keep near him, and his brother, who had come to take back his van. The group had another couple of days' tomb spotting to do, and I decided to go along with Uruch, who asked me to accompany his brother in the van. An hour out of Konya the brother discovered the lights weren't working, and we stopped for an hour to have them fixed. Just a little incident, but it set the tone for the journey.

In the lee of a mountain we stopped at a town called Aksehir, whose most famous son had caused me to laugh for years. The jokes and stories of the fool/wise man Hoca Nasruddin have been translated into dozens of languages. Uruch led us to his tomb, holding a shaky Britta by the arm, and showed us the tablet in front of it that Nasruddin always claimed was the center of the world. When anyone challenged him to prove it, he would say, "Measure it, and you will find out." The tomb was approached from the street through a gate where a fee was due. On all other sides, however, it was open for free to the world. Hoca, I am sure, must have been the presiding spirit over this last run into Istanbul.

I don't remember which tombs Uruch had us stop at, though at one Britta fell on the pavement outside and refused to get up for twenty minutes, finally leaving her rosary there in the gutter as a token of her presence. Part of me longed to bundle her into the car, another part respected her state as being as valid as my own or anyone else's.

If we weren't stopping for a tomb it was for tea, or a phone call, to pick up some fruit, wander about a little, have a chat. We had left Konya soon after midday, it normally being an eight- or nine-hour journey to Istanbul. The lights died again on the van, and we ate *kofta* and soup while they were being fixed. By midnight I was acting as relief driver, dodging between trucks on a road thick with fog interspersed with rain. Just before the freeway the exhaust dropped off and we taxied through the toll gate, sounding like a tractor.

Half an hour down the freeway the engine sputtered, came to life again, and finally gave out altogether. We have run out of gas, the brother informs me. Out of gas at three in the morning in the middle of nowhere on the verge of a freeway with juggernauts thundering by a few inches away. I started out along the verge, hoping that Uruch had noticed what had happened, that he would be waiting somewhere up ahead. It struck me that I had never walked along a freeway at night in my life.

Suddenly I realize I am walking lightly, that however mad the situation is, however downright stupid, it is what is happening, like it or not. With this acceptance came an astonishing joy. Walking along that freeway I was suddenly, unreasonably, and entirely happy. I wasn't blind to the human frailties that had caused our difficulties, but somehow everyone felt lovable despite, even because of, their faults. I had tried to accept difficulties in the past and often felt a dullness more than anything resembling joy. But acceptance isn't putting up with, I realized now, not something that can be planned beforehand. This that I know now is a sudden crack, an aperture in the heart that sees and acts with clarity on what is before it.

What was before me was an endless road with no sight of Uruch, who was sailing on to Istanbul. When I got back to the van a breakdown vehicle had arrived, the brother having found a phone, and we were towed twenty miles to the next service station. When we finally came to a stop in Istanbul I sat up to see yet another graveyard. Surely not! No, this was just the view from the brother's house. It was seven in the morning. It had taken us nineteen hours to drive from Konya. The mad thing was, I didn't even mind.

Full
Circle

Soon after my return from Istanbul I went for a long walk down Saint Catherine's Valley. I hadn't been there in years. It was a Monday, and the hills were as quiet as I had known them thirty, forty years before. The wind blew large raindrops into my back while a pale sun struggled to break through ranks of clouds. The Court looked the same, though there was a large car outside, the balustrade had been mended, and the fishponds filled in. The notice on the gate told me I was within visiting hours for the chapel. Catherine's wheel had been removed from the porch, I noticed.

In the visitors' book were two fresh entries:

St. Catherine's revisited by a family member. Denise Strutt. Lady Strutt, her mother, perhaps, had let me play on the balustrade all those years ago.

Then, underneath her relative's entry: *I just came here because the most wonderful and beautiful rock band in the world, the Cure, recorded their latest album, Wild Mood Swings, at Jane Seymour's house, St. Catherine's Court.*

I sat under the white dove descending in stained glass, watching the dust dance in endless patterns. What a perfect symmetry, I thought. Who could ever explain the threads that had placed these two entries together: the one an epitaph for a world dissolving, the second a postmodern Cure? At that moment I knew the world to be a seamless whole. Sliman's radio in the heart of the Sinai, running out of gas on a Turkish highway, the feeling of awe in the vastness of the Sahara, the sight of an old woman with a gold crown on her head——every moment was asking me to awaken to the secret design of my life hidden to my own daylight eyes. Unique for every person, the cast of a soul has an unspeakable intelligence. That's it! That is the truly sacred, I thought: the intelligence in every human heart that longs to know itself in the light of the world.

Useful Addresses

DIVINE NEW YORK

The Cathedral Church of Saint John the Divine, 1047 Amsterdam Avenue,
New York NY 10025
Telephone: (212) 316-7400

SAHARA: THE FRUITFUL VOID

Sahara Tours, Youf-Ahakit, B.P. 207, Tamanrasset (Hoggar), Algeria

THE GANGES AND THE CITY OF LIGHT

H. W. L. Poonja, 20/144A Indira Nagar, Lucknow, Uttar Pradesh 226016

THE WAY OF THE ANIMAL POWERS

Oliver's Camp, P.O. Box 425, Arusha, Tanzania, East Africa
Telephone: (255) 057-3108; fax: (255) 057-8548

RUMI: TURNING FOR LOVE

Center for Studies in Central Asian Music, A.3924 Schloss Rosenau,
Niederneustift 66, Austria
Telephone: (43) 2822-58463; fax: (43) 2822-584-4818

FOR FURTHER REFERENCE

Personalized sacred journeys in America can be organized by Michael Eller
at First Light Journeys, 6984 McKinley Street, Sebastopol, California 95472;
email: mceller@microweb.com. Roger Housden occasionally takes small
groups on journeys to the Sahara and India. Mail can be forwarded to him by
First Light Journeys.

Credits for Epigraph Quotes

page xiii (book epigraph): Henry Miller, *The Colossus of Maroussi* (New York: New Directions, 1941).

page 1: Laurens van der Post, "Wilderness," *Lapis,* issue 2. The article was edited from a talk Sir van der Post gave entitled "Wilderness" in London in 1995, at the inauguration of the Wilderness Trust in Great Britain.

page 5: J. G. Bennett, *The Way to Be Free* (London: Coombe Springs Press, 1975).

page 37: H. L. Mencken, quoted in Jean Zimmerman and Gil Reavil, *Manhattan* (New York: Compass American Guides, 1994).

page 57: Carlo Carretto, *Letters from the Desert* (London: Darton, Longman & Todd, 1972).

page 81: The Bijak of Kabir, translated by Linda Hess (Delhi: Banarsidas, 1983).

page 105: Kathleen Norris, *Dakota: A Spiritual Geography* (Boston: Houghton Mifflin, 1993), Weather Report, December 7.

page 125: Malidoma Somé, *Of Water and the Spirit* (New York: Putnam, 1994).

page 151: Jalal al-Din Rumi, *The Spiritual Couplets,* translated by E. H. Whinfield (London: Octagon Press, 1973).